THE HUNGER MACHINE

Two week loan

Please return on or before the last date stamped below.
Charges are made for late return.

IS 239/0799

INFORMATION SERVICES PO BOX 430, CARDIFF CF10 3XT

Jon Bennett

THE HUNGER MACHINE
The politics of food

Introduction and Conclusion
by
Susan George

Polity Press
In association with Channel Four Television Company Limited
and Yorkshire Television Limited

Copyright © Yorkshire Television Limited 1987;
Introduction and Conclusion copyright © Susan George 1987

First published 1987 by Polity Press in
association with Basil Blackwell
Reprinted 1987

Editorial office:
Polity Press, Dales Brewery, Gwydir Street,
Cambridge, CB1 2LJ, UK

Basil Blackwell Ltd
108 Cowley Road, Oxford, OX4 1JF, UK

Basil Blackwell Inc.
432 Park Avenue South, Suite 1503
New York, NY 10016, USA

British Library Cataloguing in Publication Data
Bennett, Jon
    The hunger machine
    1. Famines—Case studies
    I. Title
    363.8   HC59.72.F3
    ISBN 0-7456-0444-7
    ISBN 0-7456-0445-5 Pbk

Library of Congress Cataloging in Publication Data
Bennett, Jon
    The hunger machine.
    Bibliography: p.
    Includes index.
    1. Food supply.   2. Food industry and trade.
3. Agriculture—Economic aspects.   4. Food supply—
Government policy.   5. Food industry and trade—
Government policy.   6. Agriculture and state.
    I. Title.
    HD9000.5.B449   1987   363.8   87-724
    ISBN 0-7456-0444-7
    ISBN 0-7456-0445-5 (pbk.)

Typeset in 10½ on 12pt Baskerville by Opus, Oxford
Printed in Great Britain by Billing & Sons Ltd., Worcester

Contents

Acknowledgements

The author and publishers are grateful to the following for permission to reproduce material in this book:

Cafod, the Catholic Fund for Overseas Development for 'The Arithmetic of Poverty' by Appadure, from *Just Food*.

Zed Press and Returned Volunteer Action 1979 for cartoons by Chris Welch, from *Poverty and Power*.

The author and publishers for an extract from 'What a Bewildering World' by Nazim Hizmet, from *Selected Poems* (Jonathan Cape Ltd, 1967).

Mahmood Jamal for an extract from 'Silence', from *Angels of Fire* (Chatto & Windus Ltd, 1986).

Leon Rosselson for extract from 'Who Reaps the Profits? Who Pays the Price?', from *Bringing the News from Nowhere* (Fuse Records).

East African Publishing House Limited for 'Western Civilization' by Agostinho Neto, from *When Bullets Begin to Flower* (ed. Margaret Dickinson).

André Deutsch Limited for extract from 'The United Fruit Company' by Pablo Neruda, from *Twenty Poems* (1970).

Allison & Busby Limited for 'To the Silent Majority' by Adrian Mitchell, from *For Beauty Douglas* (1982).

Preface

CHRIS BRYER

It's been called the invisible killer, the silent emergency. It is not famine and it does not make the headlines. It is the grinding poverty which, day in day out, deprives millions of people across the globe of the essentials of a decent life. In particular, they are deprived of an adequate diet. This 'normal' hunger will kill their children in their first year, destroy their health in adulthood, and take them to an early grave. More than one thousand million people are chronically hungry. Every 24 hours, 35 thousand of them die as a result.

We found that famine accounts for only a small fration of hunger-related deaths. Famines are exceptional, which is why they are news. The majority of those who die of hunger, and most of them are children, do so because they are poor. They die very quietly. They are the brothers and sisters of Alberto, who died aged six months from malnutrition and infection, because his father, a cocoa worker in Brazil, does not earn enough to buy sufficient food, let alone medicine. They are the cousins of Hassan, who died aged three months from malnutrition and TB in a hospital ward in Sudan, long after the famine had ended.

They, like us, live in a world of plenty, where more food is produced than is consumed. As Europe destroys its food mountains and America stores unsaleable grain, Brazil, Sudan, even. Bangladesh either have surpluses of their own, or are capable of producing them. People are dying, not because there is not enough food, but because they are too poor to buy it and have no land where they could grow their own.

What can we do? Perhaps the most immediate achievable change is in our own attitudes to hunger. Once it is recognized that the cause of hunger is not scarcity of food and not scarcity of land, one conclusion is that it is a scarcity of democracy: the kind of democracy which says that each person has the right to enough food.

In the end it comes down to politics. Only deep, structural changes can shift the balance in favour of the poor majority.

When famine strikes and quick action is needed, we can be good at responding, by sending the emergency aid vital in saving threatened lives.

But, as we found in making *The Politics of Food*, there is a growing body of opinion which says we need to address the wider problem.

Since it is poverty, not scarcity or natural disaster, which is the root cause of the majority of hunger-related deaths, there *are* solutions available.

Some commentators believe that these will involve radical changes in the way human beings order their affairs. But they warn that not everyone will find these changes palatable. For the poor to have the essentials to feed themselves, others must adjust to some new economic and political realities.

Introduction

SUSAN GEORGE

This book, because it is about hunger, is primarily about inequalities. Sometimes these inequalities are quite straightforward, like the obvious disparity between the rich nations and the poor. Sometimes they are hidden one inside another, like Russian dolls. But always, everywhere, they are the reason for deep-seated, persistent hunger – simply another name for injustice. This is why charity, however necessary it may be to alleviate distress, is not the relevant virtue for fighting hunger. That virtue is justice, because charity can never be more than a stop-gap – it does not and cannot change unjust structures. Injustice and inequalities are structural, and have firm foundations. Our hope is that this book will help to undermine those foundations.

Jon Bennett, who has seen hunger in Africa from the front lines, has done a remarkable job. All I want to do here is set out some of the more flagrant inequalities, as a kind of touchstone for reading his text.

One of the best indicators of hunger is the infant mortality rate, or IMR, which tells you how many children per thousand die before their first birthday. In what follows, I've combined this indicator with the 'child' mortality rate that includes children up to five. About 125 million children are born each year; some 18 million (14.5 per cent) will not see their fifth birthday. Of those who die, 97 per cent were born in what is called the 'Third World' or the 'South'. So the *first inequality* is quite obviously the one that exists between rich countries of the 'North' (which includes countries like Japan or Australia, as well as Europe and North America) and the poor South. In the same way, people in the North have a much longer life expectancy at birth (LEB) than those who live in the South.

The efforts the countries of the South have made to emerge from their poverty, part of it an inheritance from their colonial past, have been deflected or destroyed by those of the North. In the late 1960s and 1970s, there were great hopes for a New International Economic Order (NIEO) put forward by the so-called 'Group of 77', which now includes some 120 Third World nations. They hoped for fairer and more stable prices for their raw materials, open access to Northern markets for their industrial products, more aid in line with the target set by the UN (a modest 0.70 per cent annually of the rich countries' abundance) and a number of other measures that would have helped them to help themselves.

What they got was talk, talk, talk, and no action. If, instead of spending blood and treasure on meetings, preparing briefs, devoting their best brains to this international agenda, the '77' had simply invested the same sums in their own development, they would be further on their way out of the woods today. Clearly, the North never had the slightest intention of making concessions, but it expertly kept the carrot dangling in front of Southern noses for over a decade. Today, the NIEO is a cadaver. Raw material prices are lower than ever, in what looks like a permanent slump. Crushing debts compound the woes of the South. The rich countries act as if they can continue to ignore the misery of well over half the population of the planet. They exhort the poor to pull themselves up by their own bootstraps, never mind that the Third World is barefoot, and has no boots.

Most of the policies the rich world *has* practised *vis à vis* the South have been destructive for their peasantries and have worsened the hunger problem. Techniques that may work in Iowa are not a prescription for radically different societies. Strategies like the 'Green Revolution' have contributed to concentrating land in fewer hands, leaving millions with no place to go. Transnational agribusiness corporations may increase their own sales, but they also increase the price of food in countries where the majority is far too poor to buy it. Food aid may have saved some lives for a time, but it has also made countries more dependent on imports, or on further hand-outs. Huge 'development' projects have tended to benefit the elites, increasing their capacity to oppress the poor and the hungry. Sometimes, as in the case of large dams, such 'development' simply displaces thousands of peasants without compensation, and without alternatives, except migration to mushrooming cities where they find no jobs.

In spite of this grim picture, every country in the world (including the rich ones) has made at least *some* progress over the past quarter of a century in reducing infant mortality rates and increasing life expectancies. An important question for judging inequalities, thus, becomes 'By how much have things changed?' We should also ask how a given Third World country ranks compared to others that are approximately as rich, or as poor. Relative wealth is usually measured by the Gross National Product (GNP) per capita, which simply means the value of goods and services generated per person by the economy of the country in question. Figures published by the World Bank, considered the most accurate available, give the following picture for 19 rich countries of the capitalist world and 32 poor ones (for the moment, China and India are left out of the poor group, since we'll look at them later):

| | 19 Rich countries | | 32 Poor countries | |
	Infant mortality	Life expectancy	Infant mortality	Life expectancy
1960	29	70	165	41
1982	10	75	87	59
% Change	−65	+7	−47	+44

Source: World Bank, 1984.

This doesn't look too bad – except that the rich countries have made greater progress in reducing infant mortality than poor ones. IMRs in some rich countries (in Scandinavia for instance) are now considered irreducible, but some poor countries still have IMRs of over 200 per thousand births. 'Average' figures tell us very little about the condition of the poorest people, but the yawning gap between North and South is evident.

A *second inequality* often exists between two countries of the same approximate level of wealth. The cases of India and China are a good illustration. Both are very large countries whose history changed radically at the end of the 1940s – India became independent in 1947, the Chinese revolution led to the formation of a people's republic in 1949. Both started from more or less the same level of poverty and, even now, have nearly the same GNP per person. But they have pursued totally different development strategies and, today, a child has a much better chance of survival in China than in India (an adult can also expect to live much longer in China). Here is the picture in figures:

| | India | | China | |
	Infant mortality	Life expectancy	Infant mortality	Life expectancy
1960	165	43	161	41
1982	94	54	67	67
% Change	−43	+25	−59	+63

Source: World Bank, 1984.

Clearly, the way national wealth is *shared* is far more important than the overall level of poverty. Socialist countries like China are not the only ones to have made great strides in reducing IMRs and increasing LEBs, although they tend to have a better record on the whole. Small states like Singapore, Hong Kong, Cuba and Jamaica have IMRs comparable to those of the richest nations (though Jamaica's is now going up again); Nicaragua reduced its IMR by a third in four years through improved land distribution, controlled food prices for basic staples and better primary health care.

Mortality rates of well over 200 per thousand in African countries or in North-East Brazil strike us in the North as appalling, as indeed they are, but we should also look at things in a historical perspective. In New York City, during the summer months of 1892, IMRs reached 340 per thousand – half of these infant deaths were due to the malnutrition/diarrhoea syndrome. Ten years later, the IMR in that city was still 215 per thousand and in rural, upstate, New York in 1921, the IMR was a chilling 274. A French historian has calculated that in a part of northern France in the early eighteenth century, only half the people reached their twentieth birthday; between a quarter and a third of them died during their first year of life.

Whose World?

The term 'Third World' was first coined by the French demographer, Alfred Sauvy, who used *tiers monde* the way the French have always used the term *tiers état*, i.e. the 'third estate' of pre-Revolutionary France. The first estate was the nobility, the second the clergy and the third everybody else, including the bourgeoisie, artisans, tradespeople and many others who were not poor by a long sight. It's a good distinction to keep in mind these days when 'Third World' tends to evoke undifferentiated misery. Not everyone is poor there either, as this book shows in some detail.

The First World consists of developed market-economy countries represented in the Organisation for Economic Cooperation and Development (OECD). The 'Second World' is sometimes used to refer collectively to the socialist countries of the North – the USSR and its satellites.

The Second World usually gets left out of succinct discussions of hunger. While the Northern socialist countries may have rather drab, monotonous and starchy diets, even their worst enemies don't accuse them of allowing substantial numbers of their citizens to go hungry. Life expectancy figures are in the high 60s for men; the low 70s for women; slightly lower than those of capitalist countries. Infant mortality rates are a shade higher (ranging from about 11 to 19 per thousand) but there is no evidence that infant deaths should be ascribed to nutritional deficiencies.

In fact, if we can believe World Bank estimates, Eastern Europe has generally *higher* levels of 'daily calorie supply per capita' than most Western European countries. The German Democratic Republic, for example, has over 3,718 calories available per person per day; the comparable figure for the USA is 3,623 calories. There may be a lot of things wrong with these societies but significant hunger isn't one of them.

A second reason for according the 'Second World' scant attention in a 'hunger' book is that these countries do not intervene very much in Southern food systems. Indeed, one wonders what Third World leader would call upon the Soviet Union, notorious for not meeting its own agricultural targets,

continued

for advice! While the Western countries have been instru-
mental in worsening Third World food distribution patterns,
East Europeans have largely confined their (often
unsuccessful) efforts to industry, railways and the like.

Eastern Europe's trade is also largely with itself. Figures
from the UN Conference on Trade and Development
(UNCTAD) show that the Soviet bloc is responsible for only 9
per cent of world exports and 8 per cent of world imports,
compared with about 65 per cent of each for the developed
market-economy countries. Eastern Europe has some barter
agreements, but it's not much of a drain on Third World
resources. In a few cases, it may be a decided help, as when the
Soviet Union purchases sugar from Cuba at several times the
world price. The big exception here is fishing: the USSR is
second only to Japan in the catch it brings home, some taken
from Third World waters.

The major impact of the Soviet bloc on the world agricultural scene is on prices. If the USSR has an especially bad
harvest, it may jump into world markets with a vengeance.
The spectacular grain price increases of the early 1970s could
be partly ascribed to massive Soviet purchases. Since then,
however, the Russians have tended to make long-term
purchasing arrangements, and this has smoothed out the ups
and downs of the market for other buyers.

The *third inequality* strikes rural, as opposed to urban people.
Statistical evidence on this point is fairly thin, but every time a
survey does try to measure urban/rural IMRs in the Third World, it
comes to an identical conclusion – rural people are worse off. The
World Bank has been saying for years that 90 per cent of the world's
hungry people live in the countryside. This may change as migration
to cities picks up speed, but it is paradoxical that those who produce
food, or who *could* be producing food, are the first to suffer from the
lack of it.

A huge study of West Bengal in India, covering 50,000
households, showed that some rural areas had IMRs approaching
210 per thousand – a far cry from the World Bank's global figure for
India of 94 cited in the table above. There's a good reason for such

'urban bias'. Most governments give city people preference, and make sure they have access to soup-kitchens or food-ration shops in times of shortage. This is because the governments themselves want to survive: history has shown over and over that urban people get very upset when food is in short supply, and can easily turn into revolutionary mobs! Rural people, on the other hand, are usually dispersed and poorly organized, and, if need be, the army can prevent them from reaching the seat of power in the cities.

But whether people live in the country or the city, the hungry ones among them will be subject to a *fourth inequality*, based on their social class. In all the pictures of famines we've seen over the past several years, not one has shown a Third World army officer, or cabinet minister or rich shopkeeper starving to death! Hunger is reserved for the poor, because contrary to what many people believe, even in times of famine *there is usually plenty of food* nearby, at a price. It is this price the poor cannot afford.

Villages, like towns, have class differences and the rank a person occupies will determine how much she or he does or does not eat. Most peasants in the world still rely on 'self-provisioning' for their food consumption – they grow what they and their families eat. This is no longer true in the West. Although farming families in richer countries may raise some vegetables or animals for their own consumption, they certainly don't make flour out of their own wheat – they sell their crop and buy their bread from the bakery or the supermarket like everyone else.

In the Third World, fewer and fewer peasants now have enough land to insure themselves a year-round food supply, and many who are classed as 'peasants' are actually landless and must rely on wage labour for their livelihood. The Indian study in West Bengal mentioned above is instructive on social inequality in the villages too. The researchers had the good sense to look at village infant mortality rates not in the aggregate but *according to occupation*, or class. Farmers without off-farm incomes were at the top of the scale, because that classification generally indicates a family with enough land to live off comfortably all year round. Next, came farmers *with* off-farm income (meaning they had to make ends meet with paid employment); then farm labourers (mostly landless) and finally the 'self-employed' or artisans, shopkeepers, etc. What the study found was that families in the group of farm labourers' families had *significantly higher* IMRs than any other category.

Similar conclusions surface every time inquiries make an effort to link food consumption to social status – the problem is that lots of governments do not want to have this kind of data produced. One South American country discovered the findings of such a study were so bad that the government suppressed them. Researchers do not get funds for carrying out such work.

The reason that labourers fare so poorly is not only that they have no land to grow their own food; they also may be able to find work only at peak agricultural periods, sometimes only at sowing and harvest times. So their income is highly irregular. The often desperate situation of landless labourers brings to mind another factor that contributes enormously to hunger. Though not exactly an inequality in itself, it does reinforce and exacerbate all the other inequalities, particularly those that hit rural families hardest. This is the *seasonal dimension*.

Those of us who live in towns *notice* the seasons, naturally, but we're not *dependent* on them. We know we'll find the same loaf of bread in the shops in June or January. Not so the poor Third World peasant. The occurrence of hunger and of the illnesses largely due to hunger are not smooth, even, phenomena; when plotted on a graph of the year, they show high peaks and deep valleys.

Malnutrition, illness and death are far more likely to strike during the lean months that precede the harvest, or during the rainy season when food stocks may be at their lowest and food prices at their highest. People may be required to work hardest in the fields just when they have the least energy. Women, who do so much of the agricultural work, often have to stop breast-feeding their babies just when the rains increase the dangers of infection. In many rural societies, the final months of pregnancy and births occur during the hungriest months, simply because more conceptions take place after harvest when food is more abundant and people feel good! From Bangladesh to Africa, all the available research shows that IMRs are worst at the end of the rainy season and in the pre-harvest period. Such seasonal cycles are just one of the vicious circles to which the poor fall victim. A mother, poorly nourished herself, who has to make a maximum work effort at the end of her pregnancy, may give birth to a premature or underweight infant. She has trouble breast-feeding, or breast-feeds at the further expense of her own health, so she has less time and energy with which to meet her children's needs.

No wonder women and children, especially female children, are the first casualties of hunger. Indeed, the *fifth inequality* is based on gender. Women are biologically tougher than men, doubtless because nature wants to safeguard the uterus for future generations. But social structures, especially in the Third World, make quick work of destroying the advantage nature confers on women. Two illiterate people out of every three are women. Women work two-thirds of all the hours worked in the world, but they get only one-tenth of the income and own a mere one-hundredth of the property. In one study, the International Labour Organisation (ILO) identified seventeen different agricultural tasks and determined that, in Africa, women did fourteen of them.

Globally speaking, because of their relative biological weakness, more boys than girls die during their first year of life. But in a great many societies, more baby girls die than boys, since boys are systematically given more food than their sisters – especially when there's not enough to go around to begin with. Even pregnant and nursing mothers get less food than their menfolk. Again, it's hard to get accurate numbers on food distribution inside families, but the work that has been done reveals glaring female inequality. One study done in Bangladesh showed that small boys got 16 per cent more food than girls; men between 15 and 45 got 29 per cent more than their wives. This can only contribute to the vicious hunger cycle.

What about the survivors? A *sixth inequality* awaits them and it is perhaps the most morally revolting of all. Children who are *seriously* malnourished during their final weeks in the womb and in their first crucial months of life will be permanently damaged; they will be unable to realize their genetic potential physically or mentally even if, by some miracle, they are well-fed later on. The same children whose physical stature is puny and weak will be apathetic in play and learning, and thus embody – for entirely *social* as opposed to genetic reasons – the curse of hunger their whole lives long.

From the family to the village, to the national and the global level, inequalities pervade the lives of the poor and create hunger in a world where there is *more than enough* food produced for everyone. On New Year's Eve in France, people sometimes toast each other in jest saying, 'It's better to be rich and in good health than poor and ill'. As we've seen from this short description of the inequalities that are the root causes of hunger, it's *even better* to be male, white, living in a city in a rich country as a member of the upper class; than female, black, living in the countryside in a poor country as a labourer – at least if you want to stay alive for a while, with all your faculties intact!

1

The Creation of Hunger

Decide mother,
who goes without.
Is it Rama, the strongest
or Baca, the weakest
who may need it longer
or perhaps Sita?
Who may be expendable.

Decide, mother, kill a part
of yourself
as you resolve the dilemma.

Decide, mother
decide. . .
and hate.

Appadure (Indian poet), *The Arithmetic of Poverty*

We do not need to be reminded of what is meant by real hunger. Modern communication has allowed us at least a glimpse of the horror and grief of recent disasters: Biafra in the 1960s, Cambodia in the 1970s, Ethiopia in the 1980s – such places have themselves become descriptive terms for human suffering on a massive scale. When famine becomes a newsworthy 'event', television, more than any other medium, brings the hungry and wretched into our homes. And with self-conscious irony, the tools of twentieth-century 'progress' allow the rich to witness at first hand the death of the poor.

But famine slips from the headlines very quickly. So, perhaps, it should for famine is, in spite of the prominence given it in the mid-1980s, a relatively rare event. More enduring is the kind of hunger that persists year in and year out amongst the poorest people in the world. This is a silent hunger, an unremitting, chronic condition of life for an estimated half a billion to one billion people on earth, depending on whether you use the definition of the Food and Agriculture Organization (FAO) or that of the World Bank. Whatever the number, this scale of suffering usually goes unrecorded, forming a backdrop to what has become acceptable as 'normal' life.

The figures of human devastation resulting from this 'silent' hunger are staggering: 14–18 million of us die every year; 35,000 each day; 24 each minute, 18 of whom are children under five years old. No other disaster compares with the outrage of world hunger. The number of people who die as a direct result of malnutrition is equivalent to dropping a Hiroshima bomb *every three days.*

Set against this harrowing catalogue of human misery is the startling fact that there is more than sufficient food currently available to feed every man, woman, and child on the planet. In fact, the world now produces *too much* food; a surplus that lines the pockets of the rich at the expense of the poor. Humanity has begun to suffer an increasingly bad conscience; world food stocks have climbed to an all-time high at a time when global hunger intensifies. And the victims are not always in the 'poor countries'. The spectre of breadlines and soup kitchens – and even starvation – in some of the richest countries of the world, which hoard surplus food, is an ironic reminder that it is not food shortage, but an absolute shortage of political morality that humanity faces as it approaches the twenty-first century.

The problem of hunger is usually easier to define than its solution. When thousands of sunken-faced and exhausted 'hunger' refugees poured into Sudan from Ethiopia in 1985, international aid workers soon collated thick files of information on the incidence of hunger, the most vulnerable groups, and how to alleviate their immediate suffering. It was known, for instance, that malnutrition is a deficiency in essential nutrients, and that diarrhoea and dysentry often exacerbate the effects of undernourishment, especially in young children. It was also noted that men and male children were often better provided for than women.

But how do people come to be in such an appalling condition, stripped of basic human dignity and now wholly dependent on hand-outs from white foreigners under a battery of clicking cameras? The simple answers – ignorance, plain misfortune, the weather – can no longer be acceptable. 150 years of colonial and post-colonial exploitation of the Third World, and our knowledge of the political processes that weigh heavily on the shoulders of ordinary women and men, leave no room for complacency. If human poverty and hunger are so persistent, their causes must be found in the institutions, policies and ideologies which serve to widen the gap between rich and poor. People die of hunger because they are poor, because they cannot afford to buy what food is available. They lack access to basic resources. In short, they are the powerless within a system of injustice.

Social justice is not only a question of recognizing who goes without. It is a question of identifying the causes of poverty in the world, and some of the forces that resist its eradication. Those who allow hunger to exist are, in fact, in contravention of fundamental human rights. The huge collection of covenants, declarations and charters that make up the body of international law include articles that state unequivocally that 'everyone' has a right to food. Freedom from hunger, then, is a political issue, a question of human rights, just as freedom from torture is. The human rights approach is, of course, rarely taken up in any legislative sense, but should be born in mind when we look critically at how national and international economic and political systems operate, and the degree to which they infringe upon the most basic requirements of human beings.

In this book we shall be returning again and again to the question of justice at international, national and even personal levels. If people go hungry it is because their family, their boss, their government, or someone else's government promote policies that create that hunger. At the level of macroeconomics, it is international trading systems – tariffs, commodity prices, quotas, and monopolies – that have kept poor countries at the mercy of the rich industrial world. This has been compounded by Northern governments' policies on aid and military strategy, and the manner in which our declining industry has been 'protected' from competitors. We cannot hope to uncover the root causes of hunger until we appreciate the degree to which economic policies pursued by wealthier nations undermine the development of poorer nations.

There is a danger, however, of giving too much emphasis to these macroeconomic factors. Ever wary of charges of ignorance, prejudice or, even, racism, we tend to concentrate solely on what 'we' do to 'them' – and thus fall into an exaggerated, somewhat patronizing attitude. True, macroeconomics provides the *context* for world poverty but, at the level of microeconomics, hunger is perpetuated by landlords, 'middlemen', money lenders and cultural preferences towards menfolk. Moreover, governments themselves all too often annex benefits of economic growth for a small powerful elite, showing scant concern for the welfare of their own people.

Each of these issues could be the subject of a book in itself. What we have done here is to take, by way of example, certain countries, sectors of society and, indeed, individuals, whose welfare has been undermined at various levels by economic forces outside their control. The 'developing world' is an obvious starting point, for here hunger presents itself as an overwhelming, endemic problem. Hunger has become more widespread as these countries uncritically adopt 'development' strategies of the North. But, if we are looking at models promoted by the industrial North, the question arises as to whether they are appropriate even in their countries of origin. High levels of unemployment in Europe, and North America's farming crisis coupled with surprising levels of poverty and malnutrition, suggests otherwise.

The North-South divide is a simple way of describing how the world divides into rich and poor countries. The countries of the North are mostly industrial market economies (the *First* World) and non-market economies (the *Second* World), countries that are still the major consumers of *raw materials* (food, minerals, oil, cotton) produced in the South. Wealth is not evenly distributed between Northern countries, but their average Gross National Product (GNP) per capita is in excess of US$11,500, compared with only US$755 for countries of the South.[1] Nations of the South are variously referred to as developing countries or the *Third World*.

A convenient method of comparing *economic* and *human* stress, and seeing how, on a global level, the North has such an advantage over the South, is to use two related ways of measuring prosperity – GNP and infant mortality rate (IMR). GNP refers to the total value of goods and services produced within a country; IMR refers to the number of children per thousand who die in the first year of their lives. 70 per cent of the world's population – the South – commands less than 12 per cent of gross world produce. In the same 70 per cent, between 50 and 200 or more children per thousand die in their first year.[2]

Behind grim statistics, maps and definitions are ordinary people: men, women and children caught in the circumstances of persistent hunger. They are the African refugees, the displaced nomads of Sudan, the slum dwellers of Brazil, the *campesinos* of Guatemala, and the women tea-pickers of Sri Lanka. About 40 per cent of the world's hungry are children; most of the rest are women.[3]

The great majority, some 90 per cent according to the World Bank, live and work in rural areas, a long way from the main centres of wealth. Many are tenant farmers or landless labourers. If they do own land, it is usually just a small plot. Poor farmers lack access to credit and to technical support that could improve production of their meagre crops. Meanwhile, cities in Southern countries are swelling rapidly, as many thousands lose their land and emigrate to the sprawling slums of Egypt, Sao Paulo or Calcutta.

The circumstances in which these people live are as varied as the many cultures of the human race; yet the hungry have one thing in common – they are all *poor*. It is poverty that starves people to death, not the callous whims of nature, nor even the stupidity of war. And the overall war against poverty is being lost: there are more hungry people in the world today than there were a decade ago.

The Poverty Trap

The year before the drought they had sold their grain as was usual to the native store. . . [The Greek merchant] sent his men around the native villages, coaxing them to sell everything they had. He offered a little more money than they had been used to getting. He was buying at half of what he could get in the city. And all would have been well, if there had not been that season of drought. For the mealies wilted in the field, the cobs struggled towards fullness, but remained as small as a fist. There was panic in the villages and the people came streaming towards the Greek store and to all the other native stores all over the country. The Greek said, Yes, yes, he had the maize, he always had the maize, but of course at the new price laid down by the government. And of course the people did not have the money to buy this newly expensive maize.

Doris Lessing, *Hunger*

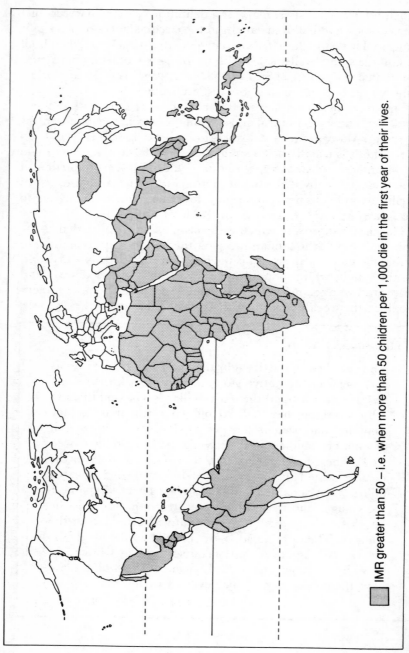

Figure 1a National Infant Mortality Rates (IMR)
Source: World Bank, 1984.

IMR greater than 50 – i.e. when more than 50 children per 1,000 die in the first year of their lives.

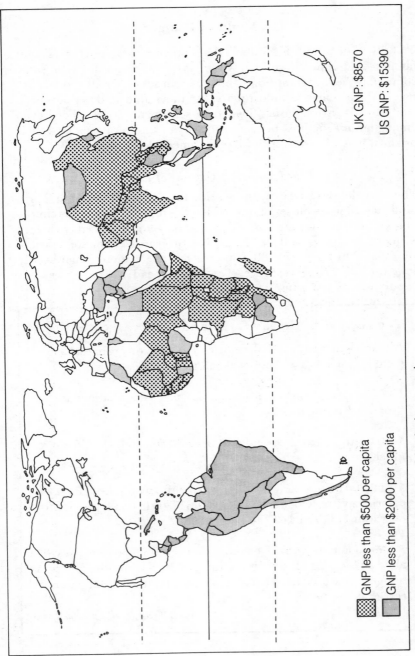

Figure 1b Gross National Products of developing countries
Source: World Bank, 1984.

GNP less than $500 per capita

GNP less than $2000 per capita

UK GNP: $8570

US GNP: $15390

The Myths of Hunger

To fully understand the systems that conspire to produce persistent hunger in the world today, we must first dispense with some commonly held assumptions about its causes. It is all too easy to regard the problem as unfortunate, but inevitable, and perhaps even God-sent. In Ethiopia in 1984, these sentiments were echoed even among famine victims themselves, many of whom rationalized their predicament with reference to 'punishment' for past sins.

The First Myth: Quantity of Food

There is plenty of food in the world. In fact, each year the world produces huge surpluses of unused food. The arithmetic is as simple as it is condemning (see box). The food *currently* produced each year is more than enough to feed the projected 6 billion people anticipated by the year 2000. Harvests have been increasing recently at a rate of 2.6 per cent yearly – well ahead of the 2 per cent population growth rate.

The Food Will Already Go Round

* There are about 3,500 calories per kilo of grain, so a ton supplies an average 3,500,000 calories.

* FAO says 2,300–400 calories a day are usually adequate for proper *adult* nutrition.

* We shall be extra careful and assume children should eat as much as adults.

* At 2,300 calories for 365 days, each child would need 839,500 calories a year, which means each ton of grain could provide for over four children (4.17 to be precise).

* A million tons would feed more than 4 million and, to provide all year long for all the 15 million children who now die from hunger, we would need to count on just about 3.6 million tons of cereal altogether.

Susan George, *Ill Fares the Land*

Since we evidently have more than enough to feed the world the problem must be one of *access*. Here again, most people of the rich North are favoured. For example, North Americans, representing only 6 per cent of the world's population, by 1978 consumed 35 per cent of the world's resources (including food) – the same as the entire developing world.[4]

The Second Myth: Overpopulation

It is true that current population densities and growth rates are unique in history. As the Industrial Revolution began, world population also began to expand rapidly. By 1800, we had reached the first billion; by 1930, the figure was 2 billion; by 1975, it was 4 billion; and, by 1987, almost 5 billion. Until very recently, the *rate* of population growth had also been on the increase, reaching almost 2 per cent by the mid-1960s.[5] That growth rate is now declining slowly, yet still there will be 6 billion people on earth by the year 2000. With a few notable exceptions, higher growth rates occur in poorer countries of the South, whereas the slowest-growing nations are all in northern Europe.

Most experts agree that uncontrolled population growth rate and density are worrying factors in the developing world. But are they, in fact, major causes of hunger and poverty? Western Europe has an average population density of about 98 people per square kilometre (with Holland having more than 1,000 per sq. km.); Africa as a whole has an average of only 18 people per sq. km. Yet the Europeans are among the best-fed people in the world and Africa suffers the highest levels of malnutrition. So there seems to be little relationship between hunger and availability of land. African countries may suffer great shortages of food, but it isn't because of a lack of land. Less than one-third of the potential arable land of this vast continent is being cultivated at present. The fact is that richer countries of the North have enough *money* to support their populations, whereas most countries of the South do not.

World hunger doesn't keep the population down; it actually keeps it up. Africa has the world's fastest population growth rate; yet this is itself an indication of prevailing poverty. Individual families will remain large as long as they lack the economic *security* we take for granted in the North. In rural areas, children are needed as workers to assure the survival of their families and to support parents in their

old age. And, since nearly one in five children born in developing countries dies before the age of five, fertility rates remain high as a safeguard.

There is a degree of 'cultural lag' in certain countries, where recent prosperity may belie the argument for more children. The Kenyan middle classes, for instance, continue to have large families; the men cannot 'hold their head high' until they have many sons. Likewise, in India, having many children is perceived as the realization of the marriage vow; for many it has little to do with their economic well-being. Where change has been most rapid, women themselves have fought to regain control of their lives and bodies. Contraception – a complex, sensitive issue when it infringes on cultural or religious mores – is not always the answer. Ultimately more significant will be the slowly changing status of women, from child-bearer to bread-winner. Obviously, women should have access to safe contraception, but only they – not foreign family planners – should make the choice.

Death by Hunger

I asked the men, 'What are you carrying wrapped in that hammock, brothers?' And they answered, 'We carry a dead body, brother.' So I asked. . . 'Was he killed or did he die a natural death?' 'That is difficult to answer, brother. It seems more to have been a murder.' 'How was the man killed? With a knife or a bullet, brothers?' I asked. 'It was neither a knife nor a bullet; it was a much more perfect crime. One that leaves no sign.' 'Then how did they kill this man?' I asked, and they calmly answered: 'This man was killed by hunger, brother.'

Josué de Castro, *Of Men and Crabs*

Death is all too common for those with little means to fall back on when the weather fails.
Jon Bennett/Andes Press Agency

In the meantime, certain governments continue to experiment with birth control methods, education and, even, sanctions. Sadly, in countries like China, there is evidence of increasing infanticide where the state's demand for one-child families conflicts with traditional preference given to male offspring. We are witnessing, in the latter half of the twentieth century, a desperate struggle between the imperative for population control and the financial and cultural backlash of millions for whom children represent continuity and security. The fundamental problem, however, must not be understated: high birth rates are primarily related to economic uncertainty. In nearly every country where malnutrition has been reduced and child death rates have decreased, birth rates have also dropped dramatically.

The Third Myth: The Weather

For many of us, world hunger became an issue for the first time when famine, in Africa or elsewhere, was causing major upheaval. It is understandable, then, that we tend to associate starvation with natural causes – droughts, floods, or earthquakes – that are beyond the control of humankind. True, it was the lack of rain in Ethiopia that ultimately pushed so many highland peasants into a state of destitution; and it was a cyclone in the Bay of Bengal that killed thousands in Bangladesh in 1985.

But, in both cases, it was the *selection* of victims that was the most revealing. No one in the USA starves when drought hits the mid-West plains, for the country has mountains of stored grain. Why, then, were no emergency food stocks available for Ethiopians? And why were the poorest Bangladeshis so desparate for land that they risked the dangerous move on to the new islands that appear every year in the Bay of Bengal?

In the Sahel, desertification is the most compelling reason for the drift of thousands from their traditional grazing land. Drought is a natural phenomenon, but its effects could have been minimized with careful planning, equitable distribution of land, and appropriate technology. Short-term commercial and political priorities have merely worsened the plight of those living in Africa's semi-arid regions. Likewise, the world's ecosystem is being dangerously tampered with in Brazil where the rain-forests are being cut down at an alarming rate. Behind each natural disaster lies a multitude of human errors that cause only the poorest people to suffer the full impact of nature. They are vulnerable to even slight changes in weather patterns, for they already live on the edge of subsistence. In high-income countries the number of people killed per disaster is less than 10 per cent of those killed in low-income countries.[6]

The Fourth Myth: The Miracle of Science

We are all familiar with the ways in which transnational companies sell the 'scientific miracle' of fertilizers, pesticides and new high-yield seeds. The scientist's laboratory is no longer contained within the confines of a university, it is now at the forefront of international competition to produce more food on less land. Population pressure and the uncertainties of the weather might have made the quest for higher productivity an incontestably beneficial project in certain countries. But in today's world technology is simply another commodity, bought and sold by those with financial power. If science is to contribute to alleviating world hunger, it must go hand in hand with social and political change.

One scientific response touted as a solution to world hunger – the Green Revolution – certainly fulfilled the promise of producing high-yield varieties of wheat and rice in certain countries of the South. Mexico provided the site for the basic research, and successful programmes were first initiated there and in the Indian subcontinent. In 1970, Norman Borlaug received the Nobel Peace Prize for breeding the first high-yield wheat varieties. The 'revolution' was born.

The Green Revolution did produce more food and enrich some farmers, but as a solution to global hunger it was an expensive failure. In most places it has widened the gulf between rich and poor and has been a cause of social upheavals in peasant cultures. In fact, not only has it failed to improve the lot of the poor, but it has also caused widespread ecological problems.

How was this possible? First, high-yield seeds require careful water management, plus high amounts of fertilizers and pesticides. Second, mechanization was, in part, a response to social problems: with less labour on the land, the problem of wages and unions could be significantly reduced. Third, the Green Revolution involved the kind of land concentration that runs contrary to basic development principles; tenants were evicted, land prices soared, and machines put many thousands out of work.

The Green Revolution

India was one of the main test beds of the Green Revolution and, within ten years, became a major exporter of cereal crops. Prosperity has, though, been disproportionate, tending to favour the already rich at the expense of poorer farmers. The state of Kerala has, to some extent, proved an exception, due mainly to more enlightened policies of the state government. The key to greater participation in the political process has been an emphasis on education, adult literacy in particular. With increasing knowledge of how their own lives fit into a world context, many Indian families in Kerala have adopted more critical attitudes to the kind of agriculture they are being urged to take up. As one farmer put it:

> I work 8–10 hours in the field and grow 70–5 per cent of the family's food. The rest we get from the government ration shops where we can get rice at market prices, which is a real improvement. Now we have hospitals and the children have a good school to go to. But I'm not so sure that things are really better than before. In the past, the children didn't get stomach ache from the pesticides. They are banned in your country, I hear. Your people send them over here instead. Usually I don't use them on my bit of land. The yield isn't quite as high, but the quality is a lot better with the old methods – like green manure – not out of a bag.[7]

Because the new techniques have become so profitable, land-owners have become direct producers themselves. Their former tenants have become seasonal wage labourers with little security of income, or have left their villages altogether.

India, once a symbol of famine, is now a net food exporter. Surely, then, there must be some enormous benefits in the Green Revolution? As a short-term expedient, it is difficult to deny that India's 'experiment' has relieved it of a dependence on food aid and imports. But poor Indians are still hungry. 47 per cent of those living in the countryside still own less than 1 acre of land, and 22 per cent own none at all. Large landholders with political power appropriate for themselves all the resources made available through government and aid organizations.[8]

The Arms Trade

The priority given to 'national security' throughout the world involves figures of staggering proportion. The money required to provide adequate food, water, education, health care and housing for each individual on earth would be about US$21 million a year. This is as much as the world spends on arms *every two weeks*.

The greater proportion (74 per cent) of the world arms bill – now standing at an incredible US$800 billion – is for the nuclear arsenals and conventional forces of the industrial North. The arms export trade totalled US$11.5 billion in 1985, two-thirds of which was destined for developing countries in the South. Politicians in Western Europe and the USA frequently boast of an era of peace through deterrence since the Second World War. But between 1945 and 1980 there were about 130 wars, in which more than 30 million people died. Most of these wars were fought in the developing South with weapons provided by the richer industrial nations of the North. The USA has been the biggest supplier, but has recently been surpassed by the Soviet Union. These are not private sales (which account for only about 5 per cent), but government to government transfers for commercial and, more importantly, political patronage.

The amount and cost of armaments from these suppliers has risen sharply in the last decade. By 1985, developing countries (including the Middle East) were spending US$7.2 billion a year on imported arms. Increasingly sophisticated weapons are now sold to the world's poorest countries. In Ethiopia in 1984, for example, the government was attacking rebels in the drought-stricken northern province with Soviet Mig-21 fighters and helicopter gunships; whilst Argentina used French-built Exocet missiles to destroy British frigates in the

continued

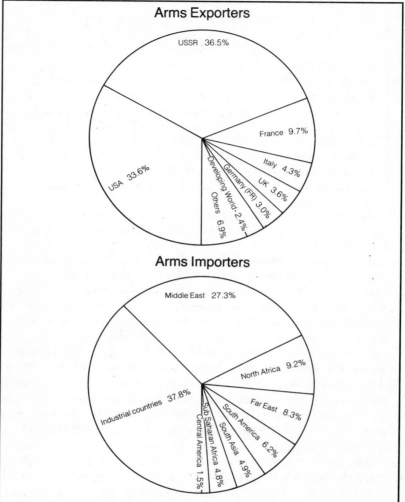

Arms Exporters

USSR 36.5%

France 9.7%

Italy 4.3%

UK 3.6%

USA 33.6%

Developing World 2.4%

Germany (FR) 3.0%

Others 6.9%

Arms Importers

Middle East 27.3%

North Africa 9.2%

Far East 8.3%

Industrial countries 37.8%

South America 6.2%

Sub Saharan Africa 4.8%

South Asia 4.9%

Central America 1.5%

Figure 2 Arms exporting and importing countries
Source: Stockholm International Peace Research Institute (SIPRI), *Annual Statistics* (1982)

Falklands War. Advanced weapon systems need careful training and maintenance; hence the superpowers have managed to extend their influence by supplying thousands of

continued

advisers and military men to the developing world.

Making comparisons between global arms spending and the plight of the starving might be a cynical exercise were it not for the fact that the amount of money involved completely overshadows the aid and development budgets of the developing South. By 1985, military spending in Northern industrial countries was more than 20 times greater than their combined overseas aid budgets. At least one scientist and one engineer in every four was employed in devising and testing new weapons systems, and some 50 million people were employed in arms industries in one way or another.

The ecological hazards of high-technology farming are only now slowly being recognized. Although the Green Revolution research institutes (like CIMMYT in Mexico or IRRI in the Philippines) are making a special effort to breed pest- and disease-resistant varieties of grain, the increasing use of herbicides, pesticides and chemical fertilizers has led to the contamination of both soil and water in many countries where these artificial products are used widely. One of the biggest problems has been the increasing immunity of insects and the fact that the natural balance of nature has been upset to such an extent that new products now have to be invented to compensate for the destruction caused by older products.

Growing more food does not, in itself, end hunger. At one level, diseases of poverty – such as dysentry and diarrhoea – contribute as much to malnutrition as actual lack of food. At another, people starve in countries where millions are spent in storing surplus food. A scientific solution to world hunger cannot, in the real world, be conducted in perfect 'laboratory' conditions. Unless it is accompanied by fair distribution to the poor farmer, equal access to land and the *means* of food production, and a careful assessment of environmental factors, it is doomed to failure. Assuming that the poor are poor because they lack certain things, some governments and aid agencies tend to focus on material redistribution – they bring in what they see as a local requirement. But material incentives invariably fall into the hands of the powerful; what the poor lack more than anything is the power to secure what they really need.

The North–South Dialogue

Dispensing with the major myths of hunger is an important step towards uncovering the real causes of the 'scandal'of hunger. In this and later chapters, examples will be drawn from a variety of different cultures and political regimes throughout the world. Common themes will emerge time and again, not least because, in spite of particular differences, it is a world *system* that ultimately determines who receives enough to eat.

The extent of world hunger is gradually receiving more attention in the world's media, and the involvement of ordinary people in the campaign for change is greater than ever before. It is a mark, however, of the fundamental weakness of this campaign that politicians of every persuasion can accommodate the 'famine movement' and sometimes even use it to their political advantage. World leaders are fully aware of the system of social injustice they have created, yet continue to fall very short of significantly changing it; for invested in the system is political and, more important, economic power.

In 1980, the Brandt Report was hailed as an enlightened and radical presentation of the issue of world hunger and underdevelopment. We should be cautious of such accolades. With its appeal to the self-interest of elites in the North, the report took for granted an economic consensus: that to shield the world capitalist economy from the worst effects of recession, greater quantities of 'aid' must pass from North to South; and that, *'focussing on questions of historical guilt will not provide answers'*.[9] It also failed to identify the real causes of inequalities *within* Southern countries, thus letting their own elites off the hook. However, the report still stands as a useful reference, particularly in respect of global inequalities:

It is not just that the North is so much richer than the South. Over 90% of the world's manufacturing industry is in the North. Most patents and new technology are the property of multinational corporations of the North, which conduct a large share of world investment and world trade in raw materials and manufactures.

Because of this economic power, northern countries dominate the international economic system – its rules and regulations and its international institutions of trade, money and finance. Some developing countries have swum against this tide, taking the opportunity that exists and overcoming many obstacles; but most of them find the currents too strong for them. In the world, as in nations, economic forces left entirely to themselves tend to produce growing inequality.[10]

Throughout the 1950s and 1960s, the UN and other national and international aid agencies directed most of their work towards increasing food production, reducing the population growth rate, and promoting the idea of a 'trickle-down' effect of economic growth – that is, that if a nation's *overall* wealth were to increase, poor people within that society would eventually benefit. But the facts have not borne this out. Brazil, now one of the richest nations in the world, has 50 million people living in extreme poverty, 40 million of whom are malnourished. Likewise, enormous disparities in wealth exist in other 'successful' countries of Latin America, Africa and Asia.

What went wrong? The UN World Food Conference in 1974 adopted views that began to show a more politically conscious perspective:

> The situation of the peoples affected by hunger and mal-nutrition arises from their historical circumstances, including social inequalities – including in many cases alien and colonial domination – foreign occupation, racial discrimination, apartheid and neocolonialism in all its forms, which continue to be among the greatest obstacles to the full emancipation and progress of the developing countries and all the peoples involved.[11]

Such statements have been echoed time and again by other international organizations, such as the European Economic Community (EEC), the Food and Agriculture Organisation (FAO) and the UN Development Programme (UNDP). Yet the analysis of the problem is rarely matched by action. This can hardly come as a surprise; economic or political change on the part of *donor* countries is usually adroitly side-stepped. There are, nevertheless, important differences between the current and previous states of establishment opinion. The Brandt Report, to some extent, typifies this change. Extreme poverty in the South is now seen as a real *threat* to the survival of the world economic system, rather than something to be

dealt with by occasional humanitarian gestures. It is this sense of
crisis, of impending economic recession and upheaval *in the North*,
that is behind reforms currently being urged upon world leaders.

In Northern countries themselves, unemployment is on the rise.
The poor who do not have access to adequate food are a relatively
small but growing minority (8–10 per cent in the USA). The slow
decline of manufacturing industries has condemned many previously rich industrial centres to a 'Third World' status, dependent upon
increasing levels of state aid.

The American Dream

The USA is the model to which poor nations are told to aspire,
yet up to 20 million people do not have enough food to eat in this,
the richest of nations. In the heart of Chicago – the capital city of
the Mid-West where most of America's food is grown – there are
250 soup-kitchens. Many thousand black people came here
from the south in search of work. For people like 23-year-old
Yollanda de Preto and her two children the 'American Dream'
has gone sour:

> There're not much jobs around here. A lot of people
> around here is on public aid. Everybody in this building,
> matter of fact, is on aid. You know, no-one in this building
> works, probably one or two people that you know have a
> nice job. . . by me having kids I have to look out for them. I
> have to go out there in the streets and beg, and I don't want
> my kids to grow up like that. I don't want them to be
> begging around people.

Feeding the World

Since there is more than enough food for each person on earth,
continuing deprivation can only be a question of access to food, and
who controls it. If economic power resides mostly in the North, then
we should not be surprised that control over world food supplies is

---

Yollanda de Preto with her two children in Chicago – she goes for her food
box each week, joining thousands like her on Welfare.
Mark Galloway

also largely in the hands of Northern countries. How does the dominant system of production and distribution operate, and who pulls the strings?

Food Production

About 1.4 billion hectares of land on earth is now under cultivation, just over half of which is in the developing South. By the early 1980s, world food production as a whole had reached unprecedented levels, giving the lie to the notion that population would soon outstrip our potential capacity to feed everyone on the planet. Taking the period 1950–80, we see how advances in agriculture and technology have affected output. In those 30 years, annual world food production actually doubled; it grew at an average annual rate of about 2.6 per cent, well ahead of the 2 per cent annual population growth rate. In the same period, the world's *per capita* food production increased by about 25 per cent.

The increase, however, has been uneven, pointing to enormous disparities between North and South. From 1950 to 1980, per capita production in the North increased by 47 per cent, but only 15 per cent in the South. In sub-Saharan Africa, food production has actually fallen by 6 per cent (15 per cent in some countries) since 1975. The same region saw a 117 per cent increase in food imports and 172 per cent increase in food aid in the last decade.

The actual quantity of staple food produced in the South is slightly less than that of the North, although the amount of land under cultivation is greater. Statistics, however, do not take account of the potential capacity for self-sufficient food production for the 85 per cent or so of the South's population who live on the land. Intensive cultivation in Europe and America may yield greater amounts per acre, but necessary capital investment is disproportionate. Moreover, intensive use of chemicals is causing long-term damage and it seems unlikely that the North can maintain current levels of output for many more years.

Three main cereal crops – wheat, rice and maize – provide the basic food for most of the world, whether directly consumed or converted into meat and dairy products. Wheat production is dominated by the Soviet Union and the USA, who in 1985–6 produced 16.5 per cent and 13 per cent of world supply respectively (although China is now the single largest producer – about 17 per

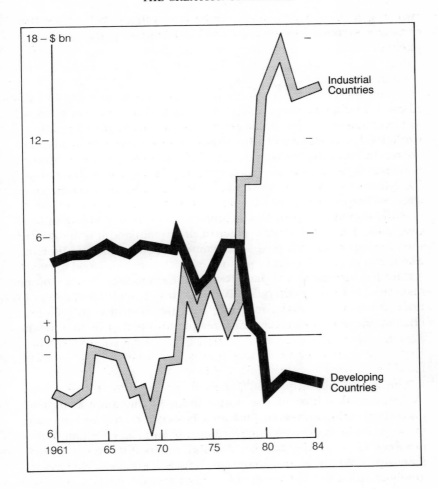

Figure 3 Value of exported food
Source: World Bank, 1984.

cent). Likewise, the USA produces about 30 per cent of world coarse grains, including maize (42 per cent).[12]

The tables are turned when we look at the third cereal crop – rice. The top five producers are all from the South with China leading the field (36 per cent) and India second (19 per cent). But these two countries have reached their goals by very different routes. India was the 'success' story of the Green Revolution, and has become highly dependent on mechanization, fertilizers and high-energy inputs. China, on the other hand, adopted a sweeping political programme involving land reform, collectivized farming and a remarkable health care system.

Grain production is not only a question of quantity, but of the amount of *energy* needed for high yields. The Chinese have depended on their single most valuable resource – human beings. Traditional dryland Asian rice culture uses only 1 calorie of energy (human labour) to produce 20 calories of rice. By contrast, modern US corn production uses 1 calorie (fuel, fertilizers, heat) to produce only 1 calorie of corn. Energy consumption for beef production is up to *20 times* this amount per calorie produced.[13]

But how much food do we actually consume? 56 per cent of total world food production takes place in the North; and it is here that a quarter of the earth's people consume more than half of its food. This is not to say that everyone in the North consumes food in excess of need. The statistics of poverty and undernourishment in Europe and the USA prove otherwise. But margins of wealth and access to food are by no means as extreme; with the exception of Russia in 1920–2, there has not been widespread famine in the North since the last century.

Cash Crops

More than two-thirds of the people living in the South draw their livelihood from agriculture, either directly as farmers or labourers, or indirectly as dependants of these groups. Even though they produce 44 per cent of the world's food, much of it is in the form of *cash crops* – that is, as raw materials, which can be exported to earn foreign capital to pay for imports.

Many governments have discovered how easy it is to increase production of export crops. They simply pay farmers more to produce, say, groundnuts than they would receive if they grew food for home consumption. They are also offered credit only for these export crops. Sadly, a country will often encourage *overproduction* in the hope of earning cash to pay for the expensive machinery and chemicals necessary to create that surplus. If farmers grow for home consumption they don't 'receive' anything. Meanwhile, the people go hungry.

The landscapes of developing countries have changed enormously in a very short space of time. Diversity in agriculture is a thing of the past; now more than ever before, these countries specialize in one or two crops for export. The result has been a wholesale destruction of traditional ways of life. Africans, Asians and South Americans now look increasingly to government marketing boards for their livelihood. Where once they grew basic subsistence crops, they now produce coffee, sugar or cotton; or even fruit, vegetables and flowers for Northern tables in the off-season.

In the 1984 drought, Zimbabwe and Kenya imported 26,000 and 39,000 tons of maize, respectively, for their hungry populations. At the same time, Zimbabwe announced a record harvest of tobacco, soya beans and cotton for export, and Kenya was exporting strawberries and asparagus to Europe. While the area under cereal or root crops in the poor countries increased by only 2 per cent since the mid-1970s, the area under coffee, sugar, and soya beans, principally for export, increased by 50 per cent during the same period.[14]

Breaking the Ecological Chain

Dependency on producing cash crops that fetch ever-lower prices can affect the environment as well as people, sometimes in bizzare and surprising ways. Bangladesh, for example, has been greatly dependent on jute as a cash-earning export. As part of its effort to diversify, the government began to promote frogs legs.

There were huge numbers of frogs in Bangladesh, and their legs are known to be a delicacy in Europe. Bangladeshi exporters of frozen frogs' legs even visited Britain, France, Italy and Germany in 1983 at the expense of the EEC aid programme. Their trade mission was a great success, but the Bangladesh frog population dwindled as they lost their legs to exports.

Only one fact was overlooked: frogs are highly efficient pest controllers, feeding on many insects that would otherwise destroy crops. Within two years, the shortage of frogs led to massive increases in destructive pests. As a result, Bangladesh now faces importing expensive and perhaps dangerous pesticides, having decimated its natural pest control.

Playing the Market

If you were to switch on the BBC World Service at certain times each day you could listen to an often confusing array of fact and figures indicating the current world price of coffee, sugar, gold, etc. These might be interspersed with phrases like the 'late chase' of tin or the 'sagging fortune' of soya beans. The information is basically for investors and speculators, but the fluctuating price of these commodities is of paramount importance to exporters in the South. Competition between countries is inevitable when so many grow the same basic export crop. Long-term economic planning in these countries is extremely difficult, since it is impossible to gauge one's export revenues from year to year. For example, in 1975 the USA bought 100 million dollars' worth of sugar from Brazil, but the following year bought none, preferring to purchase three times the usual quota from the Philippines. With nothing to fall back on, these countries are increasingly susceptible to the 'free market' trap.

Meat or No Meat?

What a bewildering world. . .
They feed people with words,
the pigs with choice potatoes.

Nazim Hizmet, Selected Poems

Vegetarians are often regarded as well-meaning cranks, but the economic argument against eating meat, particularly in Europe and North America, deserves some comment. As much as 40 per cent of the world's grain is used as cattle feed, and this includes not only feed grains (such as maize), but also one third of world food grains (e.g. wheat). On average, a family in the North will consume five times more grain (including feed grain) than a family in the South.

This is not to say, however, that if *less* grain was consumed in the North, poorer people would have more. Starvation in an era of massive world surplus has already proven otherwise. Vegetarians are on extremely shaky grounds to argue that a drop in meat consumption would be a strike against world hunger. Manioc from Thailand, soya from Brazil, and fishmeal from Peru are harvested specifically for an export (meat) market; it does not follow that, if these markets collapsed tomorrow, the poor of Bangkok, Recife and Lima would be any better off.

But in terms of energy and food distribution, the meat market demonstrates great imbalances. As well as 40 per cent of the world's grain, cattle, pigs and poultry also consume 40–50 per cent of its fish, and 25–40 per cent of its dairy produce. Pumping grain into cattle to provide prime steaks for the rich is a grossly inefficient way of using the earth's food resources. On average, 8–10 kilograms of grain and beans go to produce just 1 kilogram of meat.

Agribusiness: Profit at a Price

The world trading system is based on the buying and selling of *commodities*; oil, iron, ore, diamonds, cotton – or food. When you walk through your local supermarket you might be surprised at the huge variety of brand names from which to choose in food items. Such variety, though, is deceptive, for food commodities are being controlled by fewer and fewer giant corporations. These corporations – the transnationals – now dominate the international economic system to such an extent that Unilever, one of the largest, can modestly claim to have an annual turnover greater than the GNP of five of the poorest countries in Africa.

Since the Second World War, corporations such as Unilever have become truly transnational, in the sense that they control the whole process of food production wherever it may take place. As the the Chairman of Del Monte boasted: 'We literally begin with the seed and end at the grocer's shelf.'[15] This control and ownership has stretched to vast plantations in Africa and Asia, where the raw material for products such as soap and margarine are grown.

Once a transnational has established control of a particular sector it expands again. Not only will it directly buy raw materials from a particular country, but in the few cases when it sells the newly processed, packaged item back to this country, the price will be so much higher than that of the original raw material – that is, companies specialize in adding 'value'(cost).

Many corporations also find it more profitable to locate assembly and processing plants in countries of the South, where labour is cheap. Their motivation and success depends on continuing growth, otherwise they would be swept up by competing companies. For them, the 'market' – both consumers and producers – is literally the world, for they shift their interests from one country to another depending on how much profit can be attained from any one place.

The days of the concession company and transnational ownership of vast estates in Africa and elsewhere are drawing to a close. The commodity market has shifted; demand for food and textile products in Europe and America is now static. Nonetheless, huge corporations such as Cargill and Dreyfus still control the American grain trade; R. J. Reynolds and British-American Tobacco have huge investments in Africa and the Philippines, and Continental Grain, in Zaire.

More money is made today by those who monopolize trade and transport, rather than those who own productive land and take all the associated risks. Transnational corporations today control 85 per cent of world cocoa, 85–90 per cent of tobacco, 85 per cent of tea,

85–90 per cent of coffee, 60 per cent of sugar, 85–90 per cent of cotton, 85–90 per cent of jute, and 90 per cent of forest products. [16] . Because they have economic power, transnationals exercise powerful political influence in many developing countries. Force can be applied by making or witholding investments – quite often investments have been withheld from left-wing regimes and have expanded when right-wing ones take over.

From Debt to Violence

To understand more fully the hunger burden facing so many of the poor in the South *and* North today, we need to look back to the early 1970s, to the origin of the current debt crisis. Events in 1973 – not least the Yom Kippur War and the breaking of a major oil supply line – led to an almost ten-fold increase in the price of oil. From 1970 to 1974 it had soared from US$1.30 to US$11.00 a barrel. The organization of oil and petroleum exporting countries (OPEC) took immediate advantage of their new control of supply, and the income of Saudi Arabia, Kuwait and other oil-exporting countries rose dramatically.

But OPEC countries could not absorb the huge new-found incomes at home; they had neither the infrastructure nor the expertise. They turned to the Western banking system and invested huge sums of money there. Poorer countries of the South were, meanwhile, feeling the effects of a rapid increase in oil prices. They could no longer afford the machinery or fuel for high-technology expansion; they began to borrow heavily, not only for oil imports, but also for prestige projects, arms, and food imports. Inevitably, they turned to Western banks for substantial loans, which the banks were only too willing to provide.

Looking back, many financiers now consider that certain decisions were made in the 1970s that contravened basic principles of banking. The credit-worthiness of some countries was not fully examined and the amounts of money lent imposed a debt burden from which these countries cannot break free. For the debtor countries themselves, the only source of income was the export of raw materials – commodities whose price began to fall after 1973.

Private banks lend money for profit. Loans are usually made for a short term only, with at a floating (i.e. not fixed) interest rate.

Throughout the 1970s, all the big banks rapidly increased the proportion of profits made abroad. In 1976, for example, the American Citibank derived 13 per cent of its world-wide earnings from one country, Brazil.[17]

The rush for 'easy money' was short-lived. From 1975 onwards interest charges soured (6–17 per cent in only five years), and remained very high until the beginning of the 1980s. World recession meant that the only alternative to total bankruptcy for many debtor countries was further loans from the World Bank or the International Monetary Fund (IMF).

How does the 'debt crisis' contribute towards the underdevelopment of the South in the late 1980s? In brief, what we are seeing is a shift in the terms of domination, in the manner in which international capitalism extracts wealth from the South. There have been marked changes in the relationship between the rich and poor worlds in the last 25 years; the extraction of 'added value' from the South's raw materials has now been replaced by a parasitic demand for cash in the form of interest.

From the Second World War onwards, cash-crop economies of the South were consolidated as transnationals established their monopoly of trade in raw materials. Although that monopoly continues today, there has, since the 1970s, been a general depression of world trade as markets, particularly those in Europe and the USA, have stabilized (i.e. there is little growth). Today, international trade is characterized more by protectionist policies, trade barriers and recession.

During the period of post-war capitalist 'growth', through to the 1970s, there was, albeit in a perverse form, a link between the accumulated wealth of poorer nations and their dependency on technology, aid and trade from the North. Industrial expansion was the keyword of success; if that meant sacrificing the real value of your products to profiteering Northern companies or governments, then so be it. Southern elites, at least, would gain from such policies.

Today, however, what characterizes capitalism in its relation to the South is its totally *unproductive* nature. Debt is a means whereby dependency can still be fostered through the stranglehold of the international banking system. But who profits? Certainly not the debtor countries or, indeed, their elites, for the transfer of finance (through high interest rates and the circulation of a single currency, the dollar) does not foster industrial growth, production of goods or the creation of value. Rather, it puts profit into the hands of Northern financial institutions. This money then becomes a resource to cover the deficits and the military expenditures of the rich countries.

By 1986, Mexico owed US$100 billion, Argentina US$50 billion, and the Philippines over US$30 billion. The whole of the Northern banking system is inextricably tied to foreign debts, but in an uneven manner: thus, when inflation in industrialized countries was 3 per cent, interest rates on foreign loans were 8 and 9 per cent. It is estimated that two-thirds of Latin America's external debt has been re-exported, to be deposited in private accounts. In the last four years net transfers from the South in the form of interest payments totalled a staggering US$106 billion: Northern banks are doing very nicely, thank you!

Debt and the transfer of financial capital have had a marked effect on the economies of Northern industrial countries. The old dockland area of London, for instance, is the site for the new City, the heart of the financial servicing sector. The British government has, particularly since 1979, prioritized this sector at the expense of real production. Such a policy condemns large sections of British industry and society to 'Third World' status, dependent for their autonomy on aid and protectionist measures. Many surviving industries are now controlled by foreign companies or banks; and it seems likely that the wealth of Britain in the next century will depend not on industrial commodities, but on servicing a paper and electronic money system.

Meanwhile, the developing world's debt cannot be paid by any country without plunging it into misery and violence. When the IMF is called in to shore up a country's balance of payments with a short-term loan, certain 'adjustments' are always required. These might include a devaluation of currency, or the witholding of food subsidies. It is at this critical point that the burden of debt most directly affects the poor within these countries.

In April 1985, President Numeiri of Sudan was deposed following a series of street riots in most of the country's main towns. The IMF team, frequent visitors in the last ten years, had insisted on a further drop in government subsidies on basic foodstuffs. The people rebelled. Their underlying frustrations may have been political, but the trigger for change was, quite simply, the price of bread.

Food as a Weapon

It is a sad reflection of the world we live in that food, the most fundamental of human needs, can be regarded not only as a source of wealth for the few who control it, but also as a an ultimate weapon in the quest for world domination. We need look no further than reports of the Central Intelligence Agency (CIA) of the US government to confirm our suspicions. In 1974 they published a study entitled *Potential Implications of Trends in World Population, Food Production, and Climate*.[18] At that time, the USA dominated the world grain market (in 1986, for the first ti~ie, Europe exported more wheat than the USA, and the potential benefits were clearly spelt out:

> The world's increasing dependence on American surpluses portends an increase in US power and influence, especially vis-a-vis the food-deficit poor countries. . . In bad years, when the US could not meet the demand of food for most would-be importers, Washington would aquire virtual life and death power over the fate of multitudes of the needy. Without indulging in blackmail in any sense, the US would gain extraordinary political and economic influence.[19]

The threat to withhold food supplies from those countries that do not follow an 'approved' political line has already gone beyond mere blackmail. Food aid to Chile was drastically reduced in 1973 following the election of Salvador Allende's socialist government in 1970, but resumed when the US-backed military junta seized power in September 1973. More recently, under the guise of a 'bureaucratic hiccup', emergency food supplies from the US Agency for International Developoment (USAID) to Sudan in late 1985 were delayed while the US embassy assessed the likely nature of the incoming government.

The use of the food 'weapon' can, of course, be more subtle. During confirmation hearings as US Secretary of Agriculture in 1980, John Brock remarked, 'Food is a weapon, but the way to use it is to tie countries to us. That way they'll be far more reluctant to upset us.'[20] He certainly had a point: food aid has been so successful a marketing tool that African nations now import from the USA at commercial rates three to four times the amount of food they receive as 'aid'. Substantial foreign exchange is also spent to import wheat from Canada and the EEC. One of the central concerns of African (and other) governments is political stability in the towns; thus, catering for *urban* food tastes in Lagos, Nairobi or Freetown involves increasing dependence on expensive food imports.

The food 'weapon' can only be used against an insolvent country; in the 1980s, the most vulnerable were in Africa. Northern donors became increasingly bold in seeking to direct policies within certain countries. In Mali, food aid is tied to the goverment's satisfactory performance in instituting policy changes that major donors – including the World Bank and USAID – deem correct. This, in turn, has tied rural producers to a pattern of survival that is more and more dependent on those linkages between national elites and international financiers. In neighbouring Niger in 1982–3, the government was required by major donors to sell off its grain reserves (maintained against possible shortages) in order to repay its debts to French banks. The full tragic impact of this move was not felt until the onset of famine in 1985.

As we have seen, issues of justice for the poor refer not only to the supply and demand of essential commodities, but also to access to those commodities. Even given an equitable *world* system, there would still be the question of equal access to food *within* each country. Sadly, the 'weapon' of food comes into play here also. For example, in 1984–5 the Ethiopian government consistently denied the offer of a free passage of relief food to rebel-held areas in the north of the country. This resulted in the exodus of almost half a million Tigrayans and Eritreans from their homes to the refugee camps of Sudan. Twelve months later, thousands of hungry people in southern Sudan faced the same dilemma as relief supplies were used as 'bait' by both government and rebel forces.

Any book that attempts to address the issue of world hunger and its causes risks oversimplification, particularly where the North–South dichotomy is used. We return again and again to the notion of a dominant North-based economic system that has, over a period of time, been 'incorporated' into the South. But here we deal only with general themes, not with historical particularities, or with a country-by-country analysis. The process of 'incorporation' has, of course, not been universal or even. The colonial penetration of Africa, for instance, cannot be fully understood without reference to the level of development of the *colonizer*. The Portuguese involvement in Mozambique (and its legacy) was very different from that of the British in Kenya. This should not, however, cloud the basic issue: that the exploitation of the colonies and the continuing drain on their resources has set the scene for a *global* system of inequality that favours Northern capitalist-industrial centres.

Almost all countries of the South have now attained political independence. Most, however, are far from being economically independent; their freedom of manoeuvre is restricted to a greater or lesser degree by their ties – military and economic – with the North. Some have followed World Bank-IMF advice to the letter, and have aimed for greater integration into the dominant capitalist system. The result has been impressive growth rates, but wider income disparities between rich and poor. Others have attempted, with measured success, to break free; but the price has been economic and political isolation. In the following chapters we shall consider examples of both, bearing in mind various notions of what constitutes *development*. The terminology of North–South provides a convenient shorthand for conducting a discussion of external relations – trade, investment and finance. It is important, however, that we go beyond generalized concepts, to look at the effects of particular policies on ordinary men, women and children, and on particular social classes. Only then can we make clear links between Brazil's landless and Britain's unemployed, or between Sudan's struggling nomads and bankrupt farmers in the USA.

2

Sudan: Fortunes and Famine

Let my silence speak out. . .
The silence of deep deserted eyes
and pitch black tears.
The silence of moonlight
over the shanty towns.
The silence
inside a gun's mouth
when the bullet has flown.
The silence
of a child's twisted belly
and his old eyes.

So that the dark
can be discovered
So that the silenced
are not forgotten
Let my silence be loud.

Mahmood Jamal, *Silence*

Only 15 minutes' bus ride from the well-groomed gardens of Khartoum's Hilton Hotel is the sprawling mass of shanty dwellings that have become commonplace in one of Africa's most rapidly expanding cities. Here, the population spills into areas hitherto thought of as uninhabitable. Hastily erected huts of discarded sacks, corrugated tin and cloth have pushed the city's frontiers a further 5 kilometres into the dusty void of the northern desert.

If one were to look for a single indicator of the extent of Sudan's disaster, it would be this: that the desert nomads themselves – those who have always survived the rigours of subsistence – are moving ever closer to the cities.

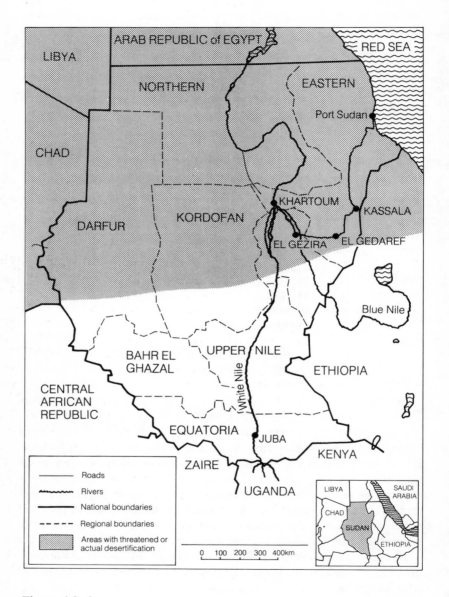

Figure 4 Sudan

For some, the stay will be temporary, a scramble for food or for a meagre salary before returning to their families in the hinterland. For most, though, this is the end of the road. Three years of drought have decimated their herds, and the few remaining crops cannot sustain them without the added income from goats and camels. There is now little choice but to begin a relentless search for subsistence on the margins of city life as occasional labourers, house girls, shoe-shine boys and, increasingly, beggars.

Sudan is Africa's largest country, covering 1 million square kilometres and with a population of 22 million. 87 per cent of these people live in the countryside, many of whom have had little, if any, contact with central government. The last five years have seen not only the worst famine this century, but also a resurgence of a long-standing dispute between the predominantly Muslim north and Christian south.

From the 'creeping' deserts of Kordofan and Darfur to the war-torn regions of Upper Nile, the Sudanese are on the move. As they spill into the shanty towns of Port Sudan or the makeshift camps of Omdurman, the townspeople 'discover' the cultural diversity of their nation, a diversity that disappears rapidly with each gust of dry wind to the north or each burst of gunfire to the south.

The Roots of Famine

The 1980s has been a decade of statistics for Africa. Never before have so many facts and figures been gathered to demonstrate the enormity of the problems facing this vast continent. Famine, the starkly visible discharge of general crisis, is no longer localized: almost without warning our attention has been drawn from the bleak wastes of Ethiopia's camps to the parched deserts of the Sudan, then further south to Kenya, Zaire and Mozambique.

Numbed by the relentless glare of publicity, few realize that this catalogue of human suffering amidst the 'silent' millions, is not a sudden, unforeseen, tragedy. Rather, it has unfolded slowly over many years. Only now has it been given prominence in the media; and only now are we being asked to look, to remember and, above all, to give.

Since 1980, development aid to sub-Saharan Africa has exceeded by ten times that given per person in Asia. Yet this, plus a host of foreign experts (reportedly more than in colonial times), has conspicuously failed to reverse the decline in agricultural production.

Sudan, in particular, has become a catalyst for development innovations: its interior is peppered with pilot projects funded, in turn, by almost every government in the Northern hemisphere. By 1985, however, experts were again locked in debate as to why this potentially abundant country – once heralded as the 'bread-basket of the Arab world' – should with such tragic irony now be suffering its worst famine this century.

Sudan's current crisis is not traceable simply to weather conditions; nor even to 30 years of mismanaged independence, though we cannot ignore the role of African elites in worsening the plight of their countrymen. Rather, it is a historical and political process at home and abroad that has set the scene for so much hardship in the 1980s. Under different circumstances, the effects of drought might only have been felt for a short period; as it is, the country is now burdened with long-term structural damage from which it will take many years to recover.

Sudan's legacy is not untypical in sub-Saharan Africa. From the time when the first slaves were carried away, the continent has been subject to tremendous disruption from outside. Africa's resources – human, mineral and agricultural – have strengthened overseas markets ever since. Where once it was slave ships, it is now planes, ships and telex machines that transfer Africa's wealth in the form of commodities and finance to the coffers of the North. Though the process may be more subtle, the argument is essentially the same: that those who control resources will always benefit by that control. And control, for most Africans, is still in short supply.

Points of View

A vast continent, located strategically between the US and the Middle East and sitting astride the sea lanes of communication between the Middle East, Europe and North America, Africa is rich in natural resources – minerals in southern Africa and petroleum in West and

continued

Central Africa. . . US interests in Southwest Asia and the
Indian Ocean have led to increased military and economic
cooperation with countries in East Africa.

The view of Africa from the US Department of State, GIST, May, 1984

The famine is upon us. We have no millet, maize, or
beans. Our cattle, sheep and goats are dead, so are our
chickens.
The women and children are hungry.
Therefore we have decided to set up our homes in this
unoccupied place. O nurturing Earth, we offer thee this
chicken; accept it, we beseech thee, and in exchange
give us bountiful harvest, numerous herds and flocks,
and many children.
Keep us free from sickness, epidemics and all evils.

Prayer of the Lobi, Ivory Coast

From Stability to Crisis

On the west bank of the Nile, about one hour's drive from
Khartoum, is the small settlement of Wadi Mansurab. The
approach is hardly encouraging: an expanse of rocky desert
punctuated only by occasional dying acacia trees or a few
sun-bleached camel bones. Not a single person is in sight. Yet like all
things of the desert, the illusion is soon dispelled. Seemingly out of
the sand itself, come streams of women and children.

Wadi Mansurab is one of the hundreds of spontaneous settlements that have pushed the frontiers of Omdurman district far into
Sudan's western desert. Though the people here have managed to
maintain a semblance of their proud independence, they, like
thousands before them, are in search of food.

In 1985, a few relief agencies responded by transporting sacks of
grain across the desert and distributing food sufficient for 2–3
months before supplies ran out. Relief organizations, however, face a
dilemma. Millions of dollars have been spent in Sudan to alleviate
the worst of the suffering, yet the permanent dislocation of
thousands is something upon which sacks of grain alone will have
little impact.

Most people in Wadi Mansurab are from the Kababish tribe,

camel-breeders from the Northern Kordofan province of western Sudan. Until recently they were self-sufficient, often wealthy, traders who sold camels as far as Egypt to the north and Nigeria to the west. But drought has decimated their herds and all that remains is occasional work on the cotton schemes of the Nile Valley, far from their traditional homeland.

More Water, More Desert

It is logical to suppose that providing more water in Sudan's deserts would help alleviate the problem of drought. Ironically, this is not always the case. In fact, the increase of water supplies, particularly from deep boreholes with diesel pumps, has actually *worsened* the disaster in Western Sudan.

Nomads usually travel hundreds of miles with their animals between seasonal water sources. Also, settled farmers have tended to rely mostly on the *wadis* (seasonal rivers) for their crops. The limit in supply has had a self-regulating effect – the environmental damage from grazing or farming is contained by the amount of water available at any one time. When supply runs dry, the nomads move on and the farmers choose alternative sites.

In the mid-1960s, the new civilian government began a 'Freedom from Thirst' campaign, which involved the digging of thousands of boreholes in the west, a political stronghold of some of the more powerful parties in the coalition. The long-term effect was that many nomads settled around the new sites, stripping land at an alarming rate and overgrazing to the point where topsoil was completely eroded in only a few years.

These boreholes have left a further legacy – a dependence on diesel to extract the water and, hence, large bills for the farmers. In the meantime, the desert is estimated to be moving southwards at a rate of 10 kilometres a year.

Water is a precious resource for nomads living in the semi-arid regions of western Sudan.
Jon Bennett/Andes Press Agency

The United Nations has estimated that at the height of the famine in the mid-1980s, 1.5 million Sudanese had been driven from their homes, 1 million were at risk of starvation, and an estimated 150 persons per day were dying of starvation.[1]

Sudan's famine, like that of Ethiopia, was not simply an ill-fated transitory event. It was not a chance misfortune bestowed upon an otherwise stable community. We have only to trace the recent history of some of the nomads of Wadi Mansurab to uncover a whole series of events that have lead to their current predicament. Each individual story may be different, but the underlying theme is one of poverty, lack of land, and systematic neglect. These people are victims of decisions to organize national economies in specific ways.

In discovering who makes those decisions and why, we must look at the nature of previous development programmes and the priorities that governed them. The sad fact is that the famine of 1985–6 was predicted years before it happened; the ingredients for disaster appeared, and were even written about, well in advance. In other words, *it was avoidable*.

New Victims, Old Causes

Historical evidence suggests that poor people in the now 'under-developed' countries of the South were able in the past to withstand famine far better than they can today. To a large extent, this is because in traditional societies (both North *and* South), the relationship between landowners and tenants was mutually benefi-cial; those who controlled land could not, in their own interest, allow tenant farmers to perish, for they were the producers of wealth.

Today, however, this relationship is breaking down at an alarming rate. It has been replaced by what is usually referred to as 'capitalist relations', that is, an economic system in which land, food and human labour are merely commodities bought and sold as a source of profit.

This gradual transition from self-sufficient control of land and production (however meagre) to that of unemployment and dependency is all too evident in the recent history of sub-Saharan Africa. Large-scale private farming, mechanization and cash-cropping are the means whereby these countries have entered the capitalist world economy. It is this transition, and what it means for ordinary men and women, that is the setting for Sudan's crisis in the 1980s.

The Tyranny of High Oil Prices

Sudan's dependence on oil imports has proven costly for small farmers. Let us consider the village of Sheik al Tayib, which lies on the west bank of the Nile about 40 kilometres north of Khartoum.

Most farmers here now use small diesel pumps to irrigate the land nearest the river. Until the early 1970s, most would have used oxen, but the low price of diesel was an incentive to change. Only a few years after the oil boom, prices again began to rise as the price of cotton – Sudan's major export – fell on the world market. So diesel rationing was quickly introduced.

The people of Sheik el Tayib had, in the meantime, sold their oxen and could not afford to pay for animals to replace the idle pumps. Hassan Ibrahim takes up the story:

> An ox from Omdurman now costs almost LS1,000 [US$250] which is too much for most of the people who work their small plots in this village. Sometimes we can borrow money, but to pay it back we must produce more on land which can only be watered from the river. Last year 1984, the river was very low and even the pumps that were working had to be repositioned and more pipes to be bought.
>
> I think we now live in a dying village. Almost all our young men have left for the towns or for Saudi Arabia looking for work. You can buy only *adis* [lentils], *ful* [beans] and tea in the shops today. No meat or flour, unless it is very expensive. Many of our children now have diseases because they don't eat correctly.

Sheik el Tayib is not untypical. In a desperate effort to 'modernize' and increase production, farmers have made themselves increasingly vulnerable to the economic fortunes of a country already heavily dependent on importing essential supplies of fuel, etc. In this situation, it is almost impossible to make any long-term plans at national or even local level.

Overpopulation may well be a problem in Sudan's cities, but in the nation as a whole it is not. There are far less people per square kilometre than in any country in Europe. Likewise, available land is not a problem in itself: Sudan has about 86 million fedans (acres, approximately) of arable land, of which only 20 million are under cultivation.

This last figure is worth looking at more closely. Of the 20 million cultivated fedans, 4 million are given over to irrigated cash crops (mostly cotton), and 6 million to mechanized rain-fed schemes, generally geared towards the export market. The remaining 10 million fedans are traditional farming and pasture lands; yet this is, for the most part, marginalized land, much of which lies in Darfur and Kordofan. It is no accident that these were the worst affected famine areas in the mid-1980s.

This pattern of land use, where the best land is increasingly given over to commercial farming, has mainly occurred since 1970. To understand fully what is happening today, it is worth tracing the changes that have taken place over this period.

The 1970s

We might first ask why it was that the previous drought and famine of 1970–3, which so devastated the Sahelian countries and Ethiopia, left Sudan relatively untouched. Certainly, it was not a question of weather conditions – rainfall was as bad, if not worse, as in neighbouring countries.

The answer lies not in natural causes but in the delicate balance of agricultural and economic policy being pursued by those in power and how this affects the production of grain. Throughout Sudan's colonial occupation, the British administration had encouraged the production of cotton on the largest irrigated farm in the world – the Gezira, between the White and Blue Niles. Following independence in 1956, world cotton prices fell steeply, and it became more profitable to grow rain-fed sorghum on the vast plains of western Sudan in particular.

So, large tracts of new land were acquired and the seasonal labour force multiplied throughout the 1960s and 1970s. Already, then, Sudan was moving rapidly towards being a wage-based economy. But to keep cash wage rates from rising, these labourers were paid partly in kind; this not only effectively dispensed with surplus but also ensured a reasonable distribution of grain throughout the country.

A Lost Life-Style

60 kilometres to the west of Omdurman, far into the dry, wind-swept northern desert of Sudan, is the small settlement of Abu Haruf. Once it was a trading centre for the camel trains from South Kordofan to Egypt, but today it is a village consumed by huge drifts of sand almost entirely covering the mud-bricked houses. Desertification spells more than ecological change, it also destroys traditional life-styles. Awatif Moham-med has not seen her husband for four months:

He left for Gezira to find work. I think they pay him LS2 [about US$0.50] a day. He will be able to save a little and return in January or February. For myself, I have to look after the children here. Sometimes I sell eggs or tea to travellers, but otherwise we depend on the local trader to bring food from Omdurman. These days it is very expensive, so we don't often have meat, just lentils or *ful* [beans]. I have four children. I don't 'think they will stay here, but it's the only land we have.

With the depression in cotton prices, there was no incentive for most Sudanese farmers to produce cash crops for export, as happened in the savanna zones of West Africa. At the same time, they were able, on the whole, to hold on to their tenancies and actually produce food crops on their own land. In doing so, they were protected from famine in two ways. First, by combining home produce and labour payment in kind, they could now store surplus grain. Second, by being almost self-sufficient they were protected from the ravages of inflation. Part of their land was also given over to grazing, so they could keep reserves in the form of livestock as well as grain.

So, when disaster struck for so many drought-affected Sahelian countries in the early 1970s, Sudan went relatively unscathed. But, already, the scene was set for a change of fortune in the 1980s; for those drawn into becoming wage earners were now to become

increasingly vulnerable to the changing fortunes of the national economy.

Those Who Own. . .

The 1970s was a decade of growth for Sudan. Encouraged by World Bank loans, commercial farming in the rainlands expanded three-fold and, with it, the importation of expensive machinery and chemicals. Inevitably, though, land itself came under competition as the new farms took over traditional peasant smallholdings.

Outside the big towns of Sudan, almost no land is 'owned' by anyone. The country does not suffer the problem of large landowners exploiting poor tenants, as is the case in so many developing nations. But, since the 1960s, the government has granted leases to outside business in a manner that is tantamount to actual ownership. In the 1970s, the then-socialist-oriented government of President Numeiri introduced the Unregistered Land Act, which laid down that all land was the property of the state unless formally registered otherwise. Hence, at the expense of the security of nomads and small farmers, whole areas could be appropriated by the mechanized farming sector at the stroke of an (urban, literate) pen.

Not only was time-honoured communal farmland now formally 'owned' but, also, thousands of acres of prime savanna forest and pasture were 'mined' for quick profit before they gave way to erosion. It is to the eternal shame of the World Bank that it was a major source of funding for a programme that involved the clearing of more than 5 million acres of nomadic pasture in the 1960s and 1970s.

Capital-intensive agricultural projects were initially controlled by the Mechanized Farming Corporation, established in 1968 with loans from the World Bank. Farm owners were mainly merchants or local dignitaries, those who could afford the initial outlay for equipment such as tractors.

Despite high capital costs, annual returns on a mechanized farm can ensure an income as much as 50 times that of 'traditional'

Kabish nomads in western Sudan: they are slowly losing the battle against the environment.
Carlos Reyes/Andes Press Agency

Cooperative Success

Ahmed Ghazali lives in a small village just outside Um Haraz in southern Darfur. He and his family of two wives and eight children cultivate 4 fedans (acres) of land, producing mainly rain-fed sorghum. The uncertainties of the rain mean that Ahmed often has to supplement his income by working on larger neighbouring farms. But this, in turn, means the neglect of his own land.

Finding himself in increasing debt, Ahmed resorted to using the *sheil* system – that is, the mortgaging of part of the following year's yield to a merchant willing to advance him the necessary capital to buy seeds, etc. But the terms of the loan were much steeper than the actual price of the grain produced, and Ahmed fell further into debt.

With financial assistance from an independent development agency, Ahmed and 22 fellow farmers formed a cooperative in 1985. Helped by the initial contribution they set about planting 40 fedans of land between them, some with sorghum, some with groundnuts. Each farmer contributed equal time to farming this land, whilst still retaining his individual plot.

In 1986, yields from the cooperative farm were good. For the first time, these farmers ended up richer rather than poorer. With few exceptions, they had all avoided the *sheil* system. Success stories such as this are few and far between, but demonstrate the worth of rural credit schemes at a local level as a means of overcoming the perpetual cycle of poverty.

farming. As investors and entrepreneurs, these men have preferred the kind of farming that produces maximum short-term profit, not that which is best for the land or, indeed, the people on it. In a word, the ruthless logic of capitalism has taken hold in Sudan.

. . . And Those Who Produce

Producing grain for internal consumption in the 1960s and early 1970s did not, of course, redress the imbalance of wealth in Sudan. Landowners simply accumulated wealth from an internal rather than external market. In the meantime, they created conditions for an ever-expanding seasonal labour force from as far afield as Chad to the west and Ethiopia to the east. By 1985 the International Labour Office (ILO) estimated that there were 1 million people circulating annually between their home areas and the various mechanized schemes. A further three-quarters of a million travel each year to the Gezira and Rahad cotton schemes.

Land traditionally used by peasant farmers and nomads was, through various 'edicts', passed to the commercial sector in the space of only a few years. And previous occupants of the land were now drawn into seasonal work as a main source of income. Moreover, they could no longer rely on their own means for essentials such as charcoal, skins, meat, or dairy products; these had now to be bought at the market place, requiring cash. So their demand for money, rather than payment in kind, increased.

It is here – in the fundamental shift from self-sufficiency to that of a dependent labour force – that we find the root cause of Sudan's crisis in the 1980s. Stripped of their traditional means of support, farmworkers had become simply *components of production*. In other words, they had become increasingly vulnerable to the shifting fortunes of an economy outside their control. As a seemingly limitless resource with minimal bargaining power, they could now be hired or fired at will.

More ominously, Sudanese peasants were no longer able to meet the challenge of drought. When disaster struck in 1984–5 it was not only an absolute shortage of grain that beckoned starvation for so many; it was also the fact that marginalized peasants simply lacked the means to buy what *was* available. It is the degree of purchasing power that determines who goes hungry.

Kenana

Only a few kilometres from the town of Kosti on the White Nile, is a huge irrigated sugar plantation, one of Sudan's most ambitious projects since independence. Sadly, the Kenana Sugar Refinery and Plantation has been beset by unforeseen problems.

Conceived in the early 1970s, it now produces 300,000 tons

continued

of sugar a year. Yet, given the current world surplus, the government could actually import its sugar cheaper than produce it at Kenana. When the project was started, the price of cane sugar was at an all-time high of £665 a ton; by the time the plant came into production it had plummeted to £93 a ton.[2]

The vagaries of the world market can, to some extent, be offset by obtaining quotas from certain countries or favourable trading terms under the EEC's Lomé Convention; but the cane-producing countries of the Caribbean, Africa and Pacific find it increasingly difficult to sell their produce in the face of reduced European markets. Indeed, the EEC has, itself, now become a major exporter of sugar.

Against the odds, Kenana and the country's four smaller (comparatively very run-down) companies continue to produce for most of Sudan's domestic requirements. But production costs are high: US$70 per ton is lost on depreciation and interest; and US$25 goes towards maintaining an expensive infrastructure on the site for a small privileged managerial elite. Two-thirds of the salaries of the 400 expatriate workers is paid in foreign currency, still a major drain on the company's finance. The initial feasibility study estimated the cost of the whole project at US$150 million; the final bill was US$613 million. With a majority shareholding of 42 per cent, the Sudanese government is the main loser.[3]

Yorkshire Television researchers found that only about 2 per cent of the original inhabitants of the area – the Kenanian tribe – found work on the site. Their traditional rights were apparently drastically curtailed – an agreement between the sugar company and the government meant local people could be legally evicted. They were not even allowed to extract water from the canal system.

Around the perimeter of the scheme itself are ten settlements for the 15,000 workers and their families. 50 per cent of the scheme's sugar is cut by hand. The men receive between LS10 and LS15 (US$3–5) a day for up to 12 hours' work. Unions are discouraged, though not officially banned, and most fear for their jobs. The alternatives are worse – displacement and unemployment.

This is taken to be one of Sudan's 'model' development projects.

The Sting in the Tail

Throughout the 1970s, when private rain-fed farming dominated capitalist growth in Sudan, government expenditure reached an all-time low. The agricultural sector had been taken over by transnational agribusiness; in addition, land leases were sold at very favourable terms to ex-government and ex-army officers. Arab funds in particular were used to boost production of food crops, much of which was destined for the stomachs of livestock and poultry to be exported to Gulf states.

As recently as 1980, Sudan was still being considered as a potential supplier for most of the Middle East's grain needs. The Kuwait-based Arab Fund for Economic and Social Development (AFESD) had drawn up a US$6,500 million programme involving more than 100 projects designed to meet two-fifths of the Arab world's food needs by 1985.

Meanwhile, the World Bank was pressing for an increase in cotton production again, to offset balance of payment problems. There had, until then, been some attempt to use the old British-built irrigation schemes to produce import-substitution foods such as wheat and rice. However, this was essentially an 'elite' food not destined for the open market. World Bank support for it was halted in 1978 in favour of a massive rescue plan for cotton.

A classic Third World symptom had developed in Sudan by the mid-1970s. In appropriating land for huge mechanized schemes, farmers became increasingly dependent on imported technology. To pay for it, they needed foreign currency. And the only source of this currency was the beleagured cotton industry, the returns from which were decreasing each year. The 'bread-basket' strategy was, if anything, an attempt by Sudan to rid itself of dependence on a volatile world cotton market.

The attempt failed and so, indeed, did the cotton 'revival'. Escalating oil prices, drought and trade deficits plunged Sudan into massive debt. Cotton yields themselves declined – export revenues from cotton decreased by an average 9 per cent each year from 1970 to 1976. In the same period, the demand for agricultural machinery for the sorghum fields, together with fuel and luxury consumption goods, caused the country's import bill to soar to an annual rate of 7.8 per cent.

The Decline of Cotton

Although 85 per cent of Sudan's agriculture is dependent on rain, it is the irrigated farming sector which, acre for acre, receives the lion's share of investment. The Gezira cotton scheme, with the recent Managil and Rahad extensions, forms the biggest irrigated farm in the world, covering an area of about 2 million acres.

But cotton – Sudan's single most important cash crop – is suffering from a fall in demand on the world market. In 1986, US$530 million of Sudanese cotton went unsold. As the government debates the future of cotton-dependency, it is the labourers who are most affected by the drop in fortune.

Hilat Mahgoub, a town of about 75,000, contains mostly cotton pickers of West African origin. They still retain their native languages, though many have been here for two generations. Omer Musa Saeed describes conditions:

> Our family used to be farmers in Nigeria, then settled here on the way to Mecca. Our life is uncertain now. We work on the cotton farms, sometimes also the women, and the children, though I'd rather they went to school. I earn LS2 for every bag of cotton I pick.
>
> There is a lot of risk. A couple of weeks ago the Gezira officials told us to go and pick cotton somewhere else on the Farm, but it would have meant being away for more than two weeks. We asked for an advance on salary for our families, but they refused, so we couldn't go. Some seasonal workers took our place. They are usually paid less, but they are guaranteed work by the tenant farmer who brings them.

Sudan's urban population find plenty of food in the market for those who can afford it.
Carlos Reyes/Andes Press Agency

Balance of payment difficulties continued and, by 1987, Sudan's external public debt had risen to an incredible US$11,000 million. Rising interest charges now mean that the country is paying more for servicing its debts than it is earning from exports.

Just as the extent of the country's famine was beginning to be known, international financiers arriving at Khartoum airport brought with them a series of austerity packages and stringent conditions: first, Sudan should guarantee Arab access to agricultural resources for private investment; second, they should call in the IMF.

A Heavy Load

It was this last condition that was to have direct bearing on the lives of ordinary Sudanese. The IMF's austere 'economic rescue package' included the removal of subsidies on food and other consumables, and a drastic devaluation of the currency. So imported goods became even more expensive and basic staple foods – flour, in particular, and sugar – shot up in price.

The Sudanese pound dropped in value by about one-third in the 12 months to March 1985. Further increases in the price of bread and sugar provoked riots in Khartoum, which triggered the downfall of President Numeiri the following month.

In the meantime, troops had been called out to quell unrest in the streets and many thousands of migrants from the drought-stricken interior were rounded up in lorries and transported back to the western provinces. Sudan was witnessing a 'cycle of oppression' so typical of debt-ridden countries of the South: hard currency debt leading to IMF control, provoking popular unrest, followed by military suppression, and then the demand for more cash to finance it, and so on.

These developments took place against the backdrop of a decade of political courtship with the USA. Sudan's avowedly 'left-wing' coup, which brought Numeiri to power in 1969, soon changed its political complexion following the death of Egypt's radical President Nasser in 1971. Taking his cue from Egypt's new pro-US president, Anwar Sadat, Numeiri ruthlessly suppressed his former socialist allies. He created conditions favourable for massive US and World Bank development funds made available through the 1970s. The

Sudan–US alliance, however, provoked deep resentment from many Arab countries and Sudanese nationalists – a situation which worsened with the agreement (not implemented) to dump American nuclear waste in the deserts of western Sudan in 1984. By early 1985 the Sudanese had had enough.

The Fat of the Land

It is tempting to conclude that foreign interference in Sudan's agriculture and economics is the only reason for the country's inability to feed itself. But it would be both patronizing and dishonest to ignore the role of Sudanese elites in this process of strangulation. In all social systems that conspire to produce extreme wealth at one level and extreme poverty at another, one can be sure of finding a surfeit of middlemen occupying the space in between.

People in the rural areas of Sudan have very little choice about where or when to sell what they grow. Apart from the village *souk* (market), the nearest sizeable market might be many miles away. Traders' lorries – usually diesel-run Bedfords – have carved a web of tracks to even the remotest corners of the country. The trucks are owned by richer merchants who often belong to a cartel of up to ten, and who fix the price of grain on the market. For larger quantities of grain taken to the main towns the mark-up price can be enormous. The price of a sack of grain can double or even treble by the time it reaches Port Sudan for export.

At the level of international commerce, subtle changes have occurred in the last decade. Nationalist policies adopted in the early 'socialist' years of Numeiri's regime have been systematically dismantled. It is true to say that, by 1980, the state itself was almost entirely controlled by an import-export oriented commercial class who had established themselves as agents in Sudan for big, foreign (mostly Arab), capital.

The importance of this shift in political power in Sudan cannot be overstated, for it serves to emphasize how indigenous elites have worked with international capital to exploit some of Sudan's richest resources. What has now become the dominant economic system produces and reproduces devastating poverty as a matter of routine. We should not, then, be too surprised to learn that, as famine hit the headlines early in 1985, grain was still being exported from Sudan to the Gulf states.

Pointing the Finger

Sudan has been. . . ruined economically, financially and politically by joint actions of the state bureaucracy, a national class of big and rich traders, and international agribusiness.

Report by the University of Hamburg for the FAO, July 1985

Famine and Finance

In the autumn of 1984, Sudanese newspapers carried the story of heated debates between central and regional government over the activities of the Faisal Islamic Bank in Darfur and Kordofan. Just as reports were beginning to come in of the extent of the famine in these regions, the Bank was apparently buying up large quantities of grain in lieu of interest, which Islam does not allow.

Conventional banking involves giving loans that are then paid back over a period of time. The Islamic system is uniquely different. Here the bank enters into a 'partnership' with the client. If a businessperson wishes to purchase goods or property, the bank itself will do the purchase, then sell back to the client at an inflated price. The difference in price becomes the 'interest' for the loan. In other words, instead of giving a money loan to be payed back with interest, the client must buy the goods from the bank itself.

This is not a mere technicality; for, in 1984–5, it enabled the Faisal Bank (plus other smaller Islamic banks) to buy up huge quantities of what remained of a poor harvest. The grain was then stored and sold back to merchants at inflated prices. By law, grain hoarding by individuals is not allowed; the banks conveniently found loopholes and accumulated large profits.

The Governor of Kordofan and Sudanese newspapers – particularly *Al-Sahafa* – exposed the whole issue in November 1984. The charge was indisputable, but the political implications were far more complex. The Faisal Bank is controlled by the small but extremely influential Muslim Brotherhood, headed by Hassan Abdullah Turabi, then Legal Advisor to President Numeiri. In fact, Numeiri himself had large shares in the Bank. The outcry from Kordofan was soon hushed up and it was 'business as usual'.

When Sudan's famine was declared 'official', the power of the 6 Islamic Banks in Sudan was temporarily curtailed; yet their combined capital still exceeds that of the other 15 banks in the country. The newly elected government in 1986 pledged to lessen the influence of the Muslim Brotherhood in Sudan but, unless alternative credit schemes are designed for poorer farmers the banks will continue to line the pockets of the rich. It is estimated that only 20 per cent of Sudanese have the assets or income to get credit from a bank.[4]

Coming To Terms With History

Although most African countries have had 25–30 years' freedom from direct colonial occupation, the historical legacy of this occupation is still being felt today. Africa became thoroughly integrated into the world economy during the colonial era. And just as African nationalist movements were taking root and challenging European influence on the continent, the economic aspects of colonial dependence deepened and strengthened. By the mid-1950s, almost all development plans were geared towards an external market and, with few exceptions, the new African leaders complied with this arrangement.

Along with the deliberate encouragement of export crops there was a very uneven development of the infrastructure of colonized countries. In Sudan, for example, railway tracks were laid not to connect internal markets, but to connect production centres with the port. In fact, it could be said that roads and railways were an impediment to the development of internal trade, for they syphoned off personnel and finance to serve an export economy.

The colonial administration in Sudan also left a stifling bureaucratic structure for the new leaders to deal with. By the early 1900s, the British had 'frozen' the shifting tribal structures in the country, giving political power only to favoured leaders under what was called the Native Administration. Thus they were able to 'divide and rule' whilst not directly replacing Sudanese practices.

Doctors' Dilemmas

I have been here now for five months and still none of the
medicines I have requested have arrived. The people bring
their children each day with TB, malaria, skin diseases
and eye infections, but the only thing I have in the
cupboard is asprin, eye-wash and iron tablets. Until they
can provide me with proper medicine from the Ministry of
Health there is no point in my being here. After I have
qualified I will probably join my brother in Saudia.

The speaker, Mohammed Faisal, is one of five junior graduate
doctors serving in the Rural Hospital at Wad Taktouk, 350
kilometres south-east of Khartoum. Only in recent years has
there been an attempt to move away from the Western-style
system of health care based around large regional hospitals with
little emphasis on primary health care. But even more
progressive initiatives have been inhibited by lack of basic
medicines and skilled personnel. Dedicated staff interested in
preventative care in rural areas – such as teaching sanitation –
often cannot reach their assigned areas because of lack of fuel or
vehicles. They are also inundated with curative work as a result
of poor basic facilities at village level.

A mid-level government doctor may earn only US$50 a
month, less than a quarter of the salary of an army captain. A
great many skilled doctors have left to work abroad and, of those
that remain, most are in private practice. The streets behind
Khartoum's central hospital are lined with small private clinics
used only by those who can afford to pay.

As independence approached, the colonial government set up
English-style rural councils throughout Sudan, which were
supposed to have wide-ranging responsibilities independent of
central government. But the favouritism enjoyed by some was to
lead to internal rivalry and inter-tribal conflict for years after the
British had left.

Although Numeiri's government abolished the Native Administration in 1971, little power remains vested in local government
bodies. Without any budget or significant say in the running of the

country, local councils have been powerless in addressing basic problems of environmental decay and prevailing poverty.

War and Poverty: a Deadly Mix

They came at night with sticks and guns. Our homes were burnt and some of us were killed, Men with uniforms, even young boys, drove us away. I don't suppose we'll return this time, there's so little left.

Joseph Akole told his story in an almost matter of fact way. He and his family of ten – Shilluk farmers from the southern district of Melut, Upper Nile Province – have grown used to the threat of eviction and intimidation in an area that has become the centre of government clashes with the expanding rebel force, the Sudan People's Liberation Army (SPLA).

'They' in this instance were government troops carrying out a routine 'clearing' operation in villages suspected of harbouring SPLA disidents. Yet, only two months previously, the same village was attacked in a similar manner by SPLA rebels in search of food or government informers. The Akole family, like many others from Melut, had had enough. Carrying only scanty provisions, they joined the wretched stream of displaced people moving north to the relatively safe town of Renk on the White Nile.

Reports on the extent of famine in southern Sudan have been difficult to come by. Access is extremely difficult, particularly during the rains, and the SPLA have, since mid-1985, cut almost all overland routes to this vast region.

The civil war in Sudan is reportedly costing almost US$100 million dollars a year, a severe strain on the country's beleagured economy. The war itself has its roots in political injustices dating back to the colonial era. 17 years' conflict was effectively curtailed in 1973 under the much-acclaimed Addis Ababa Accord. But discontent again escalated into armed resistance in 1983 for two main reasons: first, President Numeiri's tactical, and often crude, attempt to 'divide and rule', whereby Southern leaders and geographical areas were played off against each other whilst the north remained in control; second, the manner in which the (Muslim) northern-dominated central government passed laws that guaranteed that

some of the country's richest resources remained in the hands of the north.

This last point is worth looking at more closely. Southern Sudan has not only considerable agricultural potential but also a variety of minerals and – most vitally – oil. In 1983, Numeiri unsuccessfully attempted to redefine the boundaries between north and south so that the oil-rich area of Bentiu, the fertile lands of Renk, and various nickel and uranium fields, all fell within northern territory.

Explorations undertaken by the US-based Chevron company have confirmed that most of Sudan's significant quantities of oil lie in the south. Actual drilling is some years away, but the potential for solving Sudan's balance of payment difficulties is not to be underestimated. The flames of suspicion on the part of southern politicians were fanned considerably by the announcement of a plan to construct a pipeline from Kosti to Port Sudan in the north, and to build a refinery in Kosti.

Dissension exploded into warfare in 1983 with the formation of the Sudan People's Liberation Movement (SPLM). Significantly, the Jonglei Canal (see box) was one of the first targets: foreign workers were kidnapped and the enormous digging machine was closed down. In the meantime, neighbouring states had begun more open interference in Sudan's affairs since the breakdown of the Addis Ababa Accord. SPLA fighters were trained by Soviet-backed Ethiopia and sophisticated weapons were smuggled in from Libya. The SPLM's avowedly Marxist stance was also supported by various left-wing parties in the north.

By the time Numeiri was overthrown in April 1985, SPLM leader John Garang was in no mood for compromise. He issued a statement demanding immediate return to civilian rule and a significant degree of autonomy for the south. Sudan's one-year government, the transitional military council, managed to curtail Libyan support for the rebels but, with the new civilian coalition coming to power in 1986, there seems little likelihood of a new political solution to the war.

Excavating the Jonglei Canal: a monument to large scale, expensive, and perhaps inappropriate development.
Wendy Wallace

The Jonglei Canal

Carving a canal through Sudan's southern swamps was, on the face of it, a good idea. The swamps north of Bor fan out over an area the size of England and lose billions of gallons of water from evaporation. Both Sudan and Egypt are fast approaching their allocated quota of Nile water, so a canal would provide large amounts of extra water for irrigation.

But, in reality, the Jonglei Canal is a tribute to almost every mistake that can be made in development. Digging began in 1978, using what is believed to be the largest mobile machine in the world. The machine was already second-hand, and its technicians, spare parts and fuel immediately began to use up Sudan's precious foreign currency. In two years, it was falling way behind schedule and Sudan defaulted in its share of the payments to the French company running the project

The canal also provoked resentment in the south. Insufficient study was done to assess the environmental damage; southerners feared an invasion of foreign farmers taking prime new land; and traditional migratory routes for indigenous tribes and wild life would have been affected. In addition, many Sudanese were aware that an increase in the irrigated cash-crop sector would not only cost an enormous initial investment, but also depend on labour drawn from traditional rain-fed areas. Short-term advantages would have soon been outweighed by long-term consequences.

The machine was shut down by the actions of the SPLA at a time when its projected budget was three times that originally forecast. Without substantial foreign finance, it is doubtful whether Sudan can afford to set the wheels in motion again.

Hard-liners in the government are still pushing for all-out military victory in the south. Tactics employed include the arming of nomadic cattle breeding tribes, such as the Bagara, in an effort to neutralize popular support for the SPLA in the countryside. Such policies have had a devastating effect on the population of Upper Nile Province in particular – 'traditional' inter-tribal conflicts and cattle-raiding are now being conducted with sub-machine guns!

Southern towns and villages have always been dependent on

Muslim traders to bring essential supplies, including food, from the north, and even from as far afield as Kenya and Uganda. With land transport now at a halt, even the main towns are in a state of seige. The conflict shows little sign of resolution and aid agencies desperately trying to airlift grain to the towns are in no doubt that the famine of 1987–8 is already in the making.

Relief and Refugees

With the exception of Pakistan, Sudan is host to the largest number of refugees in the world. One in fifteen of Sudan's population is a refugee. The main bulk are from Ethiopia and Eritrea (771,000), Uganda (250,000), and Chad (121,000).[5] These figures include unprecedented numbers who arrived from 1984 to 1985 as a result of famine in neighbouring countries, notably Ethiopia.

Some – 120,000 Tigrayans, for example – have subsequently returned, but by far the greatest number have settled in Sudan over the past 20 years and have not received the attentions of aid organizations. Indeed, relief organizations have tended to concentrate most of their finance on the relatively small number of Ethiopian refugees – some 400,000 – living in designated rural 'settlements' under the auspices of the United Nations High Commission for Refugees (UNHCR).

But what of the other 1 million or so settlers scattered throughout the country? Many are Ethiopians who drifted to the ghettos of Port Sudan, Khartoum and Gedaref and are still officially designated aliens, political refugees who began to pour across the border as long ago as 1967.

In spite of Sudan's 'open door' policy and generally accommodating approach towards refugees, resentments have surfaced in recent years. There is little doubt that international relief and development funds in Eastern Sudan, in particular, have tended to be concentrated within the refugee community. The standard of primary education, for instance, is higher in the settlements than in government schools in the towns; hence competition for secondary school positions tends to favour refugee students. Likewise, qualified Eritreans compete favourably for the better-paid jobs in Gedaref, Kassala and Port Sudan.

Friction in the Camps

Mohammed Osman Ali is the Executive Officer of Wad Sherife settlement, just 18 kilometres from the Eritrean border. His concerns are typical of many Sudanese officials responsible for what has become Sudan's 'permanent' refugee community:

> The refugees can leave the camp and travel freely to Kassala. Many work in the city. They are very active in the market – we allow them to sell inappropriate food received as aid, like sardines or wheat flour. Mind you, when they sell this wheat the richer Sudanese who like wheat bread are satisfied, but the refugees then buy *dura* [sorghum] with the money. The poor Sudanese, of course, also like dura, but this action forces up the price of dura which is often in short supply – so the poor Sudanese lose out.
>
> The refugees are quite happy to work for low wages because they have the back-up help from the agencies. Also, because their family life has been fragmented by their frequent moving about, they won't have as many dependents as the Sudanese workers. Anyway, with so many people looking for work, this depresses wages.
>
> I personally have witnessed clashes between the Sudanese poor and refugees. I've had local people come here to this very camp, telling me it isn't fair that one lot of people have so much food whilst they have virtually nothing. I gave them some of the food donated to the refugees – strictly speaking, I shouldn't have done this, but what can I do?

Refugees from Tigray return home in 1986 after the worst year in their history. But how long before the next drought again pushes them over the edge?
Jon Bennett/Andes Press Agency

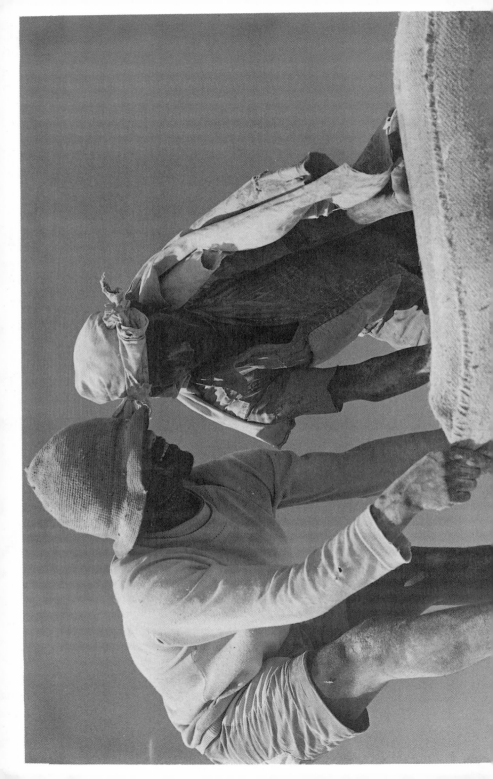

Beyond Relief: Deprivation and Dependency

In February 1986, a government official from the Managil Extension, part of Sudan's cotton belt, made a special journey to the
village of Talha in South Omdurman. His purpose was to pursuade
the 250 or so families living there to return with him to Managil for
seasonal cotton picking, just as they had done every previous year.
After five days, the official returned empty-handed; the villagers of
Talha would not be tempted, in spite of the offer of up to LS25 a day
and free transport. Their refusal to move was as straightforward as it
was disturbing: designated as 'famine' victims, they were receiving
monthly rations of grain and supplementary food from relief
agencies. As long as the free food kept coming in, there was no
reason for them to find work.

Talha is not an isolated case. It highlights the complexity of issues
surrounding 'food aid', where and when it should be used, and who
sets the agenda. Contrary to impressions created by the media, 22
million people were not starving in Sudan in 1985. Chronic famine
was localized – its effects were worst felt by particular sectors of
society in particular locations. True, drastic reductions in food
availability, inflation and large-scale displacement were to depress
the economy as a whole but, in many parts of the country, the more
naive relief agencies mistook poverty for absolute hunger, and blind
enthiusiasm took the place of professional planning.

This often resulted in the disruption of local economies as food aid
was 'dumped' on certain communities without due consideration
given to the balance of market forces in the area. Ironically, the
number of food projects underway in Sudan at the height of the
famine could not, taken as a whole, absorb the amount of money
being made available.

The issue here is more subtle than mere 'waste' – it pertains to a
cunning interplay of donor pressure, Sudanese political intrigue, and
the kind of 'aid' priorities currently being pursued. Non-
governmental agencies (NGOs) have served simply as implementing
agencies on the ground. Decisions regarding quantity of food,
targeting, and long-term commitments have been made elsewhere.
Food policy, whatever its nature, is never formed in a cultural or
political vacuum. That the USA is the single largest donor of 'aid',

In 1985–6 Sudan received its biggest-ever shipment of emergency food aid.
Jon Bennett/Andes Press Agency

military or otherwise, to Sudan, is an indication of the importance of the country in the regional balance of power.

Routine wheat imports from the USA – that is, *apart* from recent emergency supplies – amounted to almost 320,000 tons in 1985. This, together with US$190.7 million in military aid and nearly 600,000 tons of drought-food, is the price for which the USA has bought influence in the country. No one knows better than the Sudanese that there is no such thing as a free lunch.

For their part, Sudanese farmers are now facing the hidden costs of massive 'aid' imports. In 1986, the price offered for a bag of grain in Gedaref, the centre of Sudan's main sorghum-growing area, dropped to a mere LS35. Yet production cost per bag – seeds, harvesting, insecticide, etc. – was LS39. In other words, farmers were actually producing at a loss because the abundance of free grain on the market had artificially deflated prices.

There was, undoubtedly, a great need for emergency food supplies during the famine. In fact, the UN estimated an absolute shortfall of 1.5 million tons of grain in 1985, a quantity that could only be made up from immediate and urgent imports. But the relief 'machine' can often undermine carefully planned long-term strategies. It can also exacerbate existing inequalities. The greater the amount of free grain brought into the country, the less the incentive for farmers to produce. For although prices fluctuate with demand, it is the Agricultural Bank of Sudan and other national banks, to whom the farmer must sell his produce; and they set the price in accordance with what is considered acceptable to the *urban* population.

Here, we touch on one of the most crucial factors in the understanding of recent developments in Sudan. Irrespective of where the famine actually occurred, state politicians and bureaucrats were quietly determined that the *urban* population should suffer the least. As Numeiri learned to his peril, a rapid rise in the price of bread is tantamount to political suicide.

The sad fact is that because Sudan has a primarily town-oriented economy favouring a mercantile class and their respective agents, there is little personal *Sudanese* investment in small-scale agriculture, the country's only real salvation. Ironically, it is now more profitable for a land-owning person to sell biscuits in Khartoum market than it is for him to plant seeds in his home village. Until fundamental changes are made in favour of ordinary producers, they will continue to be born into, and die, in debt. Or, to use a common Sudanese expression, 'They will never taste the dollars.'

3

Aid: The Poisoned Gift?

> When I give food to the poor, they call me a saint.
> When I ask why the poor have no food, they call me a communist.
>
> Dom Helder Camara

Sunset in the village of Mukundupur, just a few miles from the River Ganges in Bangladesh; the stillness is broken only by the deep rhythmic thud of a *dekhi*, a traditional rice-mill. A young woman stands over the simple see-saw machine using her body weight as a counterbalance to the heavier end, and at a surprisingly fast pace the *dekhi* removes the husk from the paddy, and thus separates the rice grains. All that remains now is winnowing – tossing the grain high in the air as the wind removes loose chaff and dirt.

The word for 'rice' here is the same as for 'life', 'food' or 'agriculture' – an indication of its central importance in the lives of rural people. The whole cycle of rice production in Bangladesh, from planting through to storage, is labour-intensive; 80 per cent of all rice in the country is processed by hand. Crucially, it provides about 50 days' employment per year for every rural woman between the ages of 10 and 49.

But rapid changes are taking place in the name of 'aid', changes that will affect for ever the life-chances of these women on the bottom third of the socio-economic ladder. As part of a US$50 million US government grant, Mukundupur was provided with electricity a few years ago, to 'stimulate the development of rural industries'. Very soon, the *dekhi* will be replaced with a centralized power-operated mill, needing far fewer labourers. Not only will many women be out of work, but the actual quality of the rice will deteriorate. Machine-milled rice in Bangladesh is polished, and so loses a layer which is rich in vitamin-B.

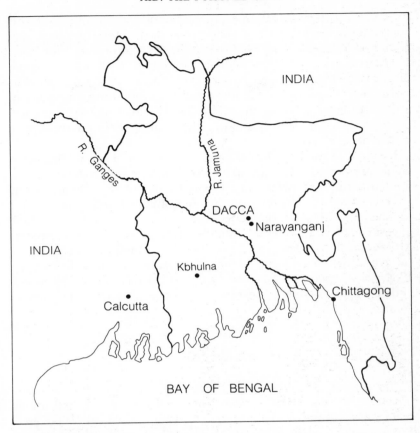

Figure 5 Bangladesh

Rural electrification is now the second largest development programme in Bangladesh. In project plans drawn up by big donors such as USAID and the World Bank, it was presumed that a by-product would be the setting up of textile and food-processing plants to provide jobs for the rural poor, 40 per cent of whom are now jobless due to increasing mechanization of traditional agricul-

---

Women working in the paddy-field – Bangladesh.
CAFOD

ture. So electrification becomes the cause and the cure. But who will constitute a market for the goods produced? Most people in the countryside are too poor even to buy basic local produce, let alone packaged processed food. When confronted with huge income disparities, corruption and poverty, aid officials are hard pushed to justify their huge commitment of funds for programmes that clearly are not directed at those most in need. Could it be that there are other reasons than simply an altruistic desire to help the rural poor of Bangladesh?

Here, as in most of the 30 poorest countries of the world, there would appear to be a large gap between the humanitarian rhetoric of foreign aid programmes and the way funds are actually allocated. Where, when, and how money is made available bears more relation to the priorities of the US or European experts and their governments than to the actual needs of the poorest people. Moreover, Bangladesh, as a low-income country, is less likely to receive substantial assistance than, say, Israel, Egypt or Turkey. In 1984, the 36 poorest countries in the world received US$4.60 per person on average; by contrast, the people of 60 middle-income countries received US$10.80 per head.[1]

What is 'Aid'?

By far the majority of the world's hungry live within the capitalist 'market', a system whose commercial and official aid institutions seem to have done little to alter the overwhelming picture of poverty. Increasingly, ordinary people have staked their hopes on aid organizations to patch up the mess that has been left by a long history of exploitation and underdevelopment. Simple humanitarian gestures – 'they are poor/hungry, we are rich/well-fed' – are now more often accompanied by a critical look at where our money goes and who really benefits from it.

'Aid' in its current usage, generally refers to a transfer of resources from governments or public institutions of the richer North to governments of the poorer South. But we should, perhaps, in the wake of the Ethiopia-Sahel drought, widen our definition to include charity contributions – private aid, which assumes greater and greater importance in the lives of the poor within developing nations. There are, then, three categories of aid.

Bi-lateral aid is the direct transfer of goods and services from one government to another. Thus, Canada might send surplus wheat to Egypt; France could send a team of doctors to Somalia; or the British government might fund a forestry project in Uganda. Bilateral aid accounts for more than three-quarters of all aid to developing countries.

Multilateral aid refers to contributions from several countries channelled through an international institution. The World Bank is the largest multilateral agency, having a 1987 budget of between US$13.5 and US$17 billion to be spent in the developing world.[2] Other multilateral agencies include the United Nations Development Programme (UNDP), the IMF, the EEC, and several regional development banks.

Private aid is that obtained directly from sponsorship or fundraising, and channelled through non-governmental/private organizations (NGOs/PVOs). Huge sums raised for disaster aid from 1984 to 1986 in many cases doubled the income of the NGOs. New organizations were also born (most notably, Live Aid), whilst others merged. But despite a disproportionate amount of recent publicity, private aid is only about one-seventh the volume of official multi- and bilateral aid. Grants by voluntary agencies can, however, often bypass bureacracy and go straight to the most needy, so dollar for dollar it can have more value than official aid.

In general, NGOs play a small but vital role in maintaining direct contact with disadvantaged groups throughout the world. Their starting point is not to treat any country as a homogenous group, but to identify certain classes or institutions in need of direct assistance, and to work alongside indigenous organizations having similar objectives. Thus, in Bangladesh, a leading British agency, Oxfam, is funding village banks and credit schemes for a range of initiatives including special lending facilities for women.

It is a sad reflection on the state of the world that the 'business' of private aid is currently thriving. The label 'private' is in some cases a misnomer: the largest NGOs in the world – for instance CARE, Catholic Relief Services and World Vision International – get large percentages of their income directly from their home governments, often as a means of sending money into areas of the world where, for political reasons, bilateral aid is inappropriate. Occasionally, private aid agencies are accused of interfering in the internal affairs of a country, or of complying too closely with the wishes of a particular regime. This has happened most notably in Ethiopia, Cambodia (Kampuchea), and El Salvador, countries where US State Department interests, in particular, are set against the perceived threat of 'communist' incursions.

Aid as a political weapon is not always covert; indeed, it could be argued that all *official* aid is simply an extension of foreign policy and a means of entrenching economic dependency. Government to government aid reinforces a diplomatic, military and political relationship; whether that aid plays a positive role depends largely on how the donor defines his national or international interest. Many countries heavily dependent on aid do not come under the usual category of 'developing' nations: Israel received US$219 per head in 1984, mostly from the USA; and in 1985 the Falklands received the equivalent of £5,500 per head from the British aid budget, while India received only 15 pence per head. Clearly, these

Nicaragua: The Aid/Trade Weapon

What happens when a small, extremely poor country adopts policies that a neighbouring superpower considers to be in conflict with its own interests? A broad-based struggle in 1978–9 to overthrow the US-backed Somoza dictatorship in Nicaragua reflected the strength of the people's desire for a more just and open society. When the Sandanistas came to power, their first priority was to put the food needs of the poor first. Radical agrarian reform redistributed 1,837,000 hectares of land between 1981 and 1985. By 1983, the area under food crops had increased by 9,089 hectares since the revolution, the main increase being in rice. Cash-crop cultivation accordingly dropped by 47,227 hectares.

But overall land use and GNP per capita has declined since the revolution, primarily because of the drain on people and finance in the war against the US-backed Contras. Damage caused by the Contras amounted to US$130 million in 1983 and US$255 million in 1984, over half the value of an average year's exports. The Nicaraguan government has had to divert human and material resources away from development into defence, which now absorbs 40 per cent of the national budget.

Efforts by the Nicaraguan government to bolster its development programme have been met by direct political intervention. In 1983, for instance, the Nicaraguan government asked the Inter-American Development Bank (IADB) for a loan to help reconstruct its fishing fleet. The US delegation demanded unusual conditions before considering the loan. The Sandanistas had to guarantee there would be sufficient fuel supplies for the proposed fishing fleet. Within weeks, the Contras had slipped ashore from a US naval vessel and blown up storage tanks at Corrinto, destroying 1.6 million gallons of oil. Fuel supplies could no longer be guaranteed and the loan was cancelled.

The Reagan administration is all too aware that military infiltration and sabotage are insufficient to topple the Nicaraguan government. Accordingly, since 1981, the USA has blocked development aid and credit to the country. A high proportion of Nicaragua's import and export trade was with
continued

the USA, and this has provided another key point of attack. In 1981, the value of exports stood at US$500 million; by 1985, it had dropped to only US$370 million. 1985 was a critical year for Nicaragua: a total embargo on trade with Nicaragua was imposed by the Reagan administration. Inflation soared from 50 to 250 per cent, and foreign debt reached an unprecedented US$4.4 million. The rationale behind the US government's attempt to strangle the Nicaraguan economy is clearly explained by the Heritage Foundation, President Reagan's Think Tank:

> Nicaraguan workers continue to have an emotional attachment to the revolutionary movement. This attachment can be expected to weaken as the economy deteriorates. . .There are some indications of growing broadly-based support to take arms to overthrow the Sandinista government, and this support could increase as further problems develop.
>
> Heritage Foundation Backgrounder, October 1980

large figures reflect political considerations, as do reductions in aid to some left-wing governments. Political considerations also influence aid spending at local levels. Helping people break out of poverty is 'development', but so too are prestige schemes such as airports, high-rise office buildings and hydroelectric dams – schemes more likely to help a country's small elite than the vast majority of the people.

So, aid is only as good as the donor, and only as good as the receiving government. It is not uncommon to find economic indicators in developing nations, such as GNP, showing favourable growth rates whilst obscuring the fact that life for millions grows worse each year. Donor governments, themselves, often proudly broadcast what they consider to be an appropriate, even generous, overseas aid budget; the small print may lead to a different conclusion. In 1985–6, for instance, British government aid grants included £65 million for providing Westland helicopters for India, and £18 million for a new repair yard to replace the naval dockyard in Gibraltar.[3]

Campaigning for a change in multilateral and bilateral aid policy means contesting the 'quality' of aid, as well as the quantity. The wealthier countries of both East and West, and most OPEC countries, have official aid budgets; these change from year to year but, in general, the amount of assistance given directly to the *poor* within countries of the South is very small in comparison to that used for political or economic leverage. The British government, for instance, allocates about 75 per cent of its bilateral budget to 'tied' aid; that is, aid given to projects that depend on the purchase of British manufactured goods (or personnel). So the money is taken from one pocket and put back into another.

Aid as a whole, however, must be put in perspective. It accounts for only 5 per cent of all invested income in the South and, set against international debt and trade deficits, its impact is limited. In 1985, an incredible 2,500 million was raised by voluntary and government agencies for famine victims in Africa. Yet, in the same year the famine-stricken countries paid back to Northern banks, governments and financial institutions *double* that amount in debt repayments. The terms of trade for basic commodities also continue to favour the rich North. In 1985, Africa would have earned an extra US$5 billion if the prices for its goods had not collapsed on the world market. By exporting their problems of recession, wealthier Northern countries have only *deepened* the crisis in the South. Juggling aid figures to make it appear otherwise is merely a face-saving exercise in the light of public concern for famine victims.

The responsibility for enduring poverty does not, of course, lie entirely on the shoulders of Northern politicians. Government and business elites of the South decide how wealth is shared among their people; all too often excessive corruption has helped to widen the gulf between rich and poor. Aid programmes have directly contributed to this process in certain countries. Military 'aid', ostensibly for 'national security' has been used to entrench ruling elites in countries where human rights are persistently violated.

After four decades of global foreign aid activity, there is now a wealth of information from which to assess its impact on development and the fight against hunger. It is impossible to deal with all these issues in one short chapter. Rather, we shall concentrate on certain aspects of the aid debate in relation to the poorer countries of the South, whose dependency on overseas assistance is most marked. In particular, we look at Bangladesh, one of the South's largest recipients of aid, where so-called development programmes have, in many instances, actually created *more* hunger and poverty. In 1980, the Brandt Report urged greater transfers of resources from North to South; if our concern is for the poorest of the poor, this simple recipe might itself be completely overturned.

Bangladesh: Aid for Whom?

The streets of Dacca, the capital of Bangladesh, are lined with elegant white government buildings left by the British in the nineteenth century. It was then that Bengal was rapidly impoverished by shifting the textile industry to Manchester, a shrewd financial decision that took no account of local people's dependency on selling their cloth to an overseas market. Some buildings have today been converted into plush hotels to accommodate the latest batch of benefactors – the aid experts who fly in from Geneva and Washington with project designs for twentieth-century prosperity.

Meanwhile, a significant proportion of Bangladesh's 100 million people are getting poorer. Corruption, 'bad aid' and huge inequalities in wealth have kept a country of rich farmland among the world's paupers. Like most nations of the South, the majority of its population (85 per cent) live and work on the land; yet 83 per cent of them live below the official poverty line. As per capita food consumption decreases, so the amount of aid pouring into the country each year increases. In 1985, Bangladesh received in excess of US$1.3 billion in aid, about half for development projects and the rest as commodity and food aid.

Since the 1971 war, followed by famine, that won Bangladesh independence from West Pakistan, the country has received more than US$13 billion in foreign aid. Each year this accounts for 50 per cent of the country's foreign exchange income and 90 per cent of its development budget. Why, then, does poverty remain as persistent and widespread as ever?

The answer lies not in technical obstacles – lack of resources, overpopulation or unproductive land – but in social and political causes. The country has been dogged by mismanagement, government corruption and violence, which threaten any tentative moves towards improving the lives of millions. Despite improved agricultural production (Bangladesh now produces more than 1 million tons of wheat, and a rice crop that outstrips the population

Experts and Bureaucrats

The Bangladesh Agricultural Development Corporation (BADC) runs farms intended to produce high-quality seed for national distribution. The farms are highly mechanized and highly 'aided'. The British government places Technical Co-operation Officers (TCOs) in many BADC farms throughout the country. It also funds various British volunteers (VSOs) to assist these nationalized corporartions with their bureacratic or research tasks.

On a typical BADC farm, there might be British trucks, Russian tractors, German combines, and Japanese machinery. Each piece of equipment is accompanied by a volunteer from the donor country, sent to look after the machines sent by their governments. With everything in place, one would expect favourable results for Bangladeshi farmers.

Sadly, these efforts are invariably wasted. First, many BADCs operate at a loss: farmers prefer to buy their seeds locally because of the low quality of BADC seeds. Second, very little maintenance is carried out on the machinery; there is a prevailing attitude that broken equipment can soon be replaced by finding another aid donor. Third, donor governments, at the same time, fund schemes that encourage a 'brain drain' from the country.

An example of this last problem lies in the British government's annual awards for about 130 Bangladeshis wishing to be trained in Britain. After completing their courses, few are willing to return to poor salaries in the homeland; indeed, the Bangladesh government itself encourages people to work abroad and send back valuable foreign exchange from which it earns millions of dollars each year. So, as the skilled, experienced, workers earn their dollars abroad, they are replaced in-country by highly paid consultants doing the work that these people should be doing. Similar patterns can be seen in industry and in the medical profession.

growth rate), poverty is on the increase. Poor income distribution is one side of the coin, the 'compliance' of official aid in ensuring that

only certain sectors of society enjoy steady growth, is the other. For our purposes, we shall see how this has affected three interrelated sectors of Bangladeshi society: the ownership and exploitation of land; the export sector (jute, in particular); and food aid.

The Squeeze on Farmers

Successive governments in Bangladesh have declared their commitment to reducing poverty and inequality by giving priority to rural development. In reality, the direct reverse has been the case. 85 per cent of the population live on the land. With irrigation and drainage, Bangladesh could produce three crops of rice per year; as it is, land is not used to its full capacity because it is concentrated in the hands of a few (often 'absentee') landlords who hire out their property to poor sharecroppers who cannot afford the necessary investments for high yields.

Sharecroppers frequently pay up to half their yields as land rent. Because they have little access to credit facilities, they can ill-afford new seed varieties, irrigation or ploughs, and few can afford to store their harvest until the prices rise later in the year. The landlords are also the local moneylenders and merchants who, thus, exercise even greater power over peasant farmers.

Bangladeshi farmers grow only around 1.35 tonnes of rice per hectare, compared with 3 tonnes in Malaysia and Indonesia. Unlike the Indian government, which has invested large amounts of money in irrigation schemes in Punjab, the Bangladesh government has decided not to spend on big irrigation projects, preferring to leave the expense to farmers themselves. But only the rich can afford the (necessary) luxury. 20 per cent of the country's cultivated land is now irrigated but, by the mid-1980s, yields were beginning to decline, and the price of farm inputs was far beyond the means of most farmers. In addition, Bangladesh rice prices fell by 8 per cent in 1985 because of extra food imports. These imports were of doubtful value to the well-being of the people, but were politically useful: by selling imported food, the government's new political party, the Jatiya, could finance itself.

Bangladesh: women and children harvesting potatoes.
Sean Sprague/CAFOD

Samata

To have no land in Bangladesh means to have no security, and to be at the mercy of landowners. The number of landless people is increasing fast. At the time of partition in 1947, when predominantly Muslim East Bengal became part of Pakistan, some land was left by Hindu landlords who fled west to India. This 'spare' land is supposed to be available to landless people. There is also new land, formed by rivers silting up with soil from the Himalayas. Known as *khas* land, this is owned by the government; but by law, the landless have a right to claim 1.5 acres of *khas* per family. In practice, it is almost always occupied by large and powerful landlords.

In an area of Pabna district, 20,000 landless people have joined together in small groups to form an organization called 'Samata' to fight for the rights of the landless to *khas* land. They have met heavy resistance, apparently from rich landowners. Tactics used against them have allegedly included false charges, looting, burning offices and houses, rape, beatings and torture. But their determination to make the project succeed is unwavering. Ghohar Ali, one of the landless, remains enthusiastic:

> At one point we were so scared of being killed that we fled from our villages and hid without food for days. But our main hope lies with Samata, so we're not going to leave. While there is one drop of blood left in my veins I will not leave Samata.

Oxfam Audio-Visuals, *Rich Land, Poor People*

Medium-income Bangladeshi farmers who were the first to eagerly take up high-yield, heavily fertilized, cultivation are now going back to low-yield varieties of crops. They are not a dwindling band. Rapid population growth and an inheritance system that divides property between all the children, has brought the average farm size down from 3.5 acres in 1977 to 2.3 acres in 1984. Farms below 2.5 acres now cover about 30 per cent of the country's cultivated area. This is not to say, however, that Bangladesh has a fair distribution of land; indeed, the *concentration* of landholdings is increasing – 10 per cent of rural households now own 50 per cent of the land. The call for land reform and an allocation to the landless is a central concern of the rural poor. More than half the entire rural population are landless.

Promoting small-scale family farming in contrast to 'Green Revolution' high-technology may seem a laudable policy for a country with an abundance of rural labour. But the changes that have taken place in the countryside are more a result of a scramble for basic subsistence in the face of spiralling costs than a positive decision to relinquish the high-tech alternative. Small farmers are at the mercy of erratic import policies, greedy middlemen and the failure of central government to uphold a price-support system. In theory, the government should buy rice and jute directly from farmers at stable prices; in practice, it is not unusual for farmers to end up selling their produce for *less* than the cost of growing it.

Aid for rural projects in Bangladesh has tended to favour those who already have access to land and the financial means to fully utilize wells, seeds, etc. Prompted by the World Bank, Bangladesh has turned increasingly to private sector industrialization on the land as well as in the towns. Large amounts of government money, supported by foreign aid, is disbursed to private enterprise. Thus, wealthier farmers in 1983–4 were able to benefit from the purchase of 40,000 shallow tube-wells and 3,500 deep tube-wells. They become wealthier in two respects: first, by achieving greater yields through irrigation; second, by monopolizing the new technology and even charging smaller farmers for its use. In direct contradiction of the aid donor's official policy, rich farmers are, therefore, able to compete directly with poorer farmers and undermine their efforts towards self-reliance.

Aid donors have been only too willing to give huge sums of money to the building of 'essential' infrastructure. In the late 1970s, USAID embarked upon a road building programme that was to cost an incredible US$133,000 per mile, roughly ten times more than the lowest cost of rural road projects in comparable countries. USAID designated this a 'Food and Nutrition' project, supposedly 'neutral' and ultimately aimed at improving trade routes for Bangladeshi farmers.[4]

In reality, those who benefit from rural roads are the larger commercial growers who can get their crops to the cities and ports more efficiently. For the rest, the roads have meant a further squeeze on finance. It is usually middlemen who buy from the poor, and who own trucks. With easier access to the countryside, they can now buy

harvested rice in the early months from a large number of scattered farmers, store it until the price rises, then often sell it back to the same farmers later in the year. A road network simply facilitates this circulation of food, to the ultimate advantage of the non-producer. It also encourages merchants from the towns to bring into rural areas luxury items that can undermine local diets.

Serving the Rich

Bangladesh has been a victim of many short-sighted notions of what 'development' entails. A classic example is the British Overseas Development Administration (ODA) funding for the Greater Dacca Power Project, an electrification programme for the capital. The scheme will cost the British tax payer £38 million (30 per cent more than was originally approved). It is the biggest ODA project in Bangladesh, justified on the grounds that improved infrastructure will encourage industry to come to the city. In the event, those who have benefited most are the middle class and foreigners in Dacca who can afford the installation fees.

The British consultants who received nearly £3 million to supervise the project, began their work in the exclusive Gulsham district where most of the rich Bangladeshis, foreign diplomats and aid workers live. A War on Want report takes up the story:

> The population density in Gulsham is around 18 people per acre, while in the Old City, where most people live, it reaches 2,000 per acre. It is said that if all the air conditioners in Gulsham were turned off, the supply of power for street lights, shops and cinemas in Old Dacca would be uninterrupted.
>
> As it is, the lights of Gulsham blaze while power is cut off in Old Dacca with monotonous regularity. The biggest British aid project, therefore, benefits only the capital, and then primarily the richer sections of Dacca's residents.
>
> Tom Learmouth and Francis Rolt, *Underdeveloping Bangladesh*

Oxen long outlive the aid-funded machinery in Bangladesh.
Tom Learmonth

Aid flows to Bangladesh have also tended to undermine local attempts at self-reliance. To ensure that the benefits of new agricultural technology reached the poorer farmers, the government's official policy has been to encourage the poor and landless to organize into cooperatives. These would share equipment and inputs, pool savings and cooperate over land and water. In the event, the exact opposite has occurred. Experience throughout the world shows that cooperative strength can only be built over a fairly long period; but the Bangladesh government, wishing to achieve quick results, has disbursed aid rapidly. Cooperatives have thus become 'leaking buckets', dominated by richer farmers who absorb the resources made available through foreign aid.

In 1976, the World Bank provided credit to the government of Bangladesh to fund 3,000 deep tube-wells (mechanically drilled wells, making possible an extra crop of rice during the dry season in the north-west of the country). The Bank's press release claimed each well would serve 25 to 50 small farmers in a cooperative group. Independent researchers found that the wells, each costing foreign donors and the government US$12,000, frequently ended up in the hands of richer farmers who themselves became the chairmen and managers of the cooperative irrigation group. They often charged their poorer neighbours for use of the wells, a cost which few could afford, and the wells were, therefore, underutilized.[5]

The World Bank's failure cannot only be measured in terms of not reaching specified 'target' groups. Democratically functioning cooperatives are unlikely ever to work in a country where landholdings are so unevenly distributed. Those who control land and resources are, in fact, the economic rival of the poor: they compete ruthlessly for every inch of ground and will use aid-financed innovations to that end. So, international donors could be said to strengthen oppressors of the poor, helping to maintain their power and authority.

Not only have large infusions of aid tended to undermine the cooperatives, they have also discouraged efforts to mobilize domestic resources. Bangladesh has one of the lowest taxation rates of any developing country. The 10 per cent of people who own half the country's farmland enjoy their wealth almost untaxed; it is politically easier for the government to raise money from foreign aid. The tax income the government *has* managed to raise comes mainly from taxes on imports, which are themselves largely aid-financed.

Political patronage has also destroyed Bangladesh's credit system. President Zia-ur-Rahman's government gave loans in return for political support in the late 1970s, but debtors are not paying back the money. Around US$500 million was handed to businessmen through government banks and financial institutions, including the Asian Development Bank and the World Bank. Only 10 per cent of the principal and interest due on industrial loans has been paid back (on agricultural loans the proportion is 25 per cent). When President Zia was killed in 1981 after some 20 coup attempts, it was thought that the incoming President Ershad would chase defaulting borrowers more thoroughly. But the loans went to people whose support the government still needs, so they have done little to encourage repayment. Lenders could take borrowers to court or seize their assets, but civil servants and judges are nervous of offending the government.

The Decline of Jute

By the turn of the nineteenth century, Bengal supplied over half the world demand for jute. In its raw form it was shipped to Dundee, where it was manufactured into cloth, sacking and rope. Since then, there has been a steady decline in demand, particularly with the introdution of synthetics, which began to compete favourably on the international market. However, jute still accounts for more than 60 per cent of Bangladesh's export earnings. Today, it is shipped mainly to Britain, the USA, the USSR and Japan with almost all international trade being controlled from London. As with so many commodities from the developing South, London merchants have the finance and access to information that enables them to speculate on the futures market, thus making long-term planning for production quotas very difficult. Sometimes orders are made, then cancelled at the last minute. Its heavy dependency on this one commodity puts Bangladesh in an inherently weak position.

Jute is grown not on large plantations like tea, but by many small farmers who rely on the annual sale of their crop. They must sell on a market which fluctuates wildly, and sometimes even destroy their unsold jute to keep prices steady. An official government minimum price is supposed to protect small farmers from the worst effects of low world prices. But this does not seem to work in practice: they are forced to sell to local merchants rather than to government warehouses. A peasant farmer explains: 'We sell our jute in the market at 60 taka. The merchants then sell it to the government warehouse at 90 taka, making a 30 taka profit for each maund [80lb]. They share this profit with the warehouse manager, giving him maybe half. So of course he won't buy from us!'[6]

Trading in Bangladesh is controlled by only a few influential families. The government invariably purchases their surplus stock rather than that of the small producer who is actually going hungry. Apart from exporting jute in its raw form, these wealthier families have also invested heavily in jute mills, especially in the late 1970s when jute-spinning was in vogue. There are 32 such mills in the country, having a capacity to produce 100,000 tonnes of cloth a year. With international demand steadily dropping, sales rarely top 40,000 tonnes, so all the mills are working below capacity. In the run up to the May 1986 elections, the government doubled wages for jute and other industrial workers; this, combined with a depression in sales, has pulled the country's industrial growth rate down to zero.

Foreign lending agencies are now reluctant to lend more money to Bangladesh's ailing industries, but still there seems a prevailing attitude of carelessness amongst Bangladeshi businessmen – past experience has taught them that, although any profit made is theirs to keep, any *loss* will be met by foreigners.

Food Aid

One of the most well-known types of foreign aid is food aid – the physical transfer of food from one country to another. Superficially, it seems an easy answer to too much food in the North and too little in the South. Unfortunately, the issue is not as straighforward as that. Only a small proportion of the world's food aid goes to disaster relief, when in most cases there are strong arguments in its favour. More often, though, it is used for long-term programmes designed for a variety of purposes, having little to do with the elimination of hunger.

During the 1960s and 1970s, there was a general assumption that population growth in the world would outstrip food production (in the event, the opposite has happened, with the world producing *more* than enough food). Prompted by the Food and Agriculture Organization (FAO), various international and bilateral

Targeting Women's Development

Women in Bangladesh have little economic power and rarely take part in any decision making. It is rare to see a woman engaging in trade of any kind. Only men go to market. Even if women grow vegetables, it is the men who sell them. Women's rights are also minimal: a man can easily divorce his wife (but not vice versa), which can leave her completely destitute, and even without her children.

Recognizing women as a disadvantaged class invariably infringes upon cultural practices and sensitivities. Real change in people's circumstances can take many years. Oxfam, a British agency, has begun to prioritize projects specifically aimed at women in Bangladesh. For instance, it is supporting a functional literacy scheme where women can learn to read and write, as well as learn basic skills in health, nutrition, poultry raising, cooperative working, and legal rights. Jute products, such as hammocks, are sold at fair prices to an Oxfam-funded organization called CORR Jute Works, which then distributes them around the world, including Oxfam trading shops in Britain.

Appropriate aid also goes to a women's organization, Ubinig, which researches, amongst other things, the Bangladesh National Drugs Policy. The issue of sterilization is of particular concern. Government-sponsored population control programmes frequently offer money (supposedly only to cover expenses) to men and women to encourage sterilization. Farida, one of the founders of Ubinig, highlights the problem:

> Some people, women in particular, accept the money only because they are hungry. They get about 175 taka, which is two weeks' wages for an agricultural labourer – and a sari when they get sterilized. How can they refuse, if their children need food or clothing? We are very concerned about this. We are talking here about poor, illiterate people who may not understand the full implications of what they are doing.

arrangements were made to cope with chronic and temporary food shortages. The US government's Public Law 480 agreement of 1954 (see box) was one of the first; more recently, the World Food Programme (WFP), the World Food Conference, and the EEC have come to the fore.

Food aid is used in three ways: for emergency purposes (famines, floods, etc.); as project food aid (assistance to particular development programmes, including food-for-work); and as programme food aid (food donated as balance of payments or budgetary support). In all its forms, food aid has accounted for only about 10 per cent of all official development assistance in recent years. In 1984–5, 25 donor countries provided 100 developing countries with 12 million tons of cereals (plus much smaller amounts of vegetables, skimmed milk powder, other dairy products, and fish). In spite of it being the 'famine year', only 5 per cent of this (660,000 tons) was for emergency assistance.[7]

The Politics of Food Aid

Large-scale international food aid started with the passing of US Public Law 480 (later called 'Food for Peace') in 1954. The aims of the original statute spelt out the clear political ramifications of disposing with grain surpluses:

> to expand international trade among the United States and friendly nations. . .to further international economic development, the expansion of US agricultural and commercial export markets. . .and make maximum efficient use of surplus agricultural commodities in furtherance of the foreign policy of the United States.

The Law also sets other limits on US food aid. Only 20 per cent of the aid is free of charge; the remaining 80 per cent is sold to the recipient country at only slightly less than market value, paid for in US dollars or a convertible currency. Alternatively, the food is exchanged for strategic raw materials required by the USA., *continued*

Women in Bangladesh rarely take part in activities or decision-making outside the home.
Sean Sprague/CAFOD

Food aid has one further characteristic: like so much assistance since the Second World War, it grew out of a desire to stop the spread of 'communism'. In the early years, it was part of the Marshall Aid plan, whereby US surpluses were sent to an ailing Europe, thus consolidating the Atlantic alliance. Later, South Vietnam was to receive large shipments right up until the USA withdrew from active involvement in the war. By 1973, almost half of all US food aid was going to South Vietnam and Cambodia. Food aid as a political weapon was particularly obvious at that time in relation to North Vietnam and Cuba. Not only was food aid to these countries out of the question, but it was also denied to any other country which traded with, or even permitted transit to, these political opponents of the USA.

Two amendments were made to the US food aid bill in 1975, to combat mounting criticism of 'political' food going to Indochina. First, it was decreed that 75 per cent of PL 480 aid must go to countries whose GNP was less than US$300 (the 1980 limit was US$625). Second, food aid should not be given to countries who consistently violated human rights.

The false assumptions of the first are clear: the GNP of Brazil is four times that of China, but a large percentage of Brazil's 135 million people are malnourished, compared with very few in China. Neither can the GNP criterion help us judge whether a recipient government will use the food aid to help the hungry. With a GNP of US$130 per capita, Bangladesh easily qualifies for PL 480 aid; its human rights violations, however, have been only too clear in recent years, and there is mounting evidence that food aid is more likely to hurt than to help the hungry. Apart from a brief, but fruitless, effort by some Congresspersons in the Carter Administration in 1977 to withold supplies, Bangladesh has received continuous, and growing, amounts of food aid.

The USA is the largest food aid donor (about 50 per cent), followed by the EEC (30 per cent), and Australia, Canada and Japan (14 per cent collectively). Distribution of food aid actually bears little relation to real need: for instance, in a normal year, about

20 per cent of all cereal aid goes to Egypt, where calorie intake per person is quite high but, by contrast, Togo, with widespread malnutrition, receives only 1 per cent of all cereal aid. Even during peak famine periods, less than 20 per cent of EEC food aid is given to famine relief. In 1985, Egypt received more EEC food aid than did Ethiopia.

The quantity of food aid is more closely related to the economic and political needs of the donors than to those of recipients. For example, US PL 480 makes explicit mention of foreign policy considerations (see box on pp. 101–2). Also, the level of food prices on the international market affects the amount made available. In 1973–4, when food was in short supply and prices were high, wheat shipments to the South amounted to only 4 million tons; only three years earlier, 10 million tons were sent.

The impact of dumping surplus food gave rise to concern towards the end of the first decade of US food aid, and the hope of correcting it was one of the motives behind the creation of the World Food Programme (WFP) in 1961. Established under the joint auspices of the United Nations and the FAO, the WFP was the first multilateral food aid agency. Food donations through the WFP, however, cannot be sold in the recipient country – it can only be used through direct feeding or food-for-work projects. WFP now handles about 25 per cent of all food aid (the current Food Aid Convention, signed in 1980, guarantees minimum supplies of 7.6 million tons a year from 22 donor countries).

Experience has shown that food aid used in normal times to supplement domestic needs can undermine local production and artificially reduce farm profits. Targeting supplies to the very poor rarely works. In Bangladesh in 1982–3, for instance, cereal food aid worth about US$160 million was distributed through the general food-subsidy scheme. About one-third of this was from the US PL 480 aid (Bangladesh is the fourth-largest recipient of US food aid). The Bangladesh government sells most of its imported food through a ration system that allows cardholders to buy a portion of their food at subsidized rates. But who receives the ration cards? While 85–90 per cent of Bangladeshis live in the countryside and many are undernourished, a mere one-third of the rationed food grains are allotted to rural families.[8] Even conservative World Bank figures confirm that a large proportion of this food never reaches those who most need it. A 1977 report stated that 27 per cent of food aid in that year found its way to the police, miltary, and civil service; 30 per cent to middle-class city dwellers; and 9 per cent to supply mills for grinding flour for urban bakeries.[9]

Bangladesh has also been a victim of 'political' aid in the same way that so many other countries in US and European 'spheres of interest' have. In the 1974 famine, the USA withdrew food aid in order to dissuade the country from trading with Cuba. More subtle pressure has also been exerted by donors wishing to impress upon the government the importance of population control. Recipients have never had the opportunity to contest the view of the major donor agencies that overpopulation rather than inequitable access to resources is the real cause of hunger in Bangladesh. President Ershad reiterated the dominant view in 1985 when he put population control as a top-priority development project. Female sterilization is central to the programme, and is again financed largely from abroad. Pressure on women to be sterilized has taken the form of threats that emergency wheat supplies will be witheld from them if they do not comply.

It is not only a question of US grain going to the wrong people or for the wrong purposes. Through the 'Title 1' agreement, the Bangladeshi government can use the proceeds from the sale of PL 480 aid for 'general budgetary support'. Food aid in the last 15 years has, therefore, directly financed a narrowly-based, unpopular military government. Revenue from the sale of rationed food provides about one-fifth of the country's operating budget; in 1978, 27 per cent of this budget went to 'defence, justice, and peace', including the militarized Special Task Force used for 'mopping up' civilian dissenters, and the holding of 10,000–15,000 political prisoners.[10]

Why Continue Aid-Giving?

Donors enthusiastically continue to pump aid into Bangladesh, despite the misuse of funds and the growing debt burden. The short-sighted belief that 'more must be better' in part explains why this has happened; but deeper reasons can be found in the link between commerce and politics. Most funds are ultimately spent in the donor countries, on equipment and expatriate salaries. Aid is, in fact, a transfer of money from Northern tax-payers to Northern private companies, passing through Bangladesh on the way. Britain's contribution to the country is a prime example: from 1979 to 1981, less than 1 per cent of the ODA's 80 million expenditure was directly spent in Bangladesh. Instead, it was used to import British goods and pay salaries to British experts.

Underlying political justification for the continuance of aid is not too difficult to find: Bangladesh lies between communist-controlled West Bengal, the highly unstable areas of North-East India, and socialist Burma. The country is, thus, an important 'sphere of influence', and aid maintains a sympathetic regime in power. British Prime Minister Margaret Thatcher explains her government's rationale for aiding poor countries in terms of East–West antagonism: 'The disparity in wealth between richer nations and the poorer. . . provides opportunities for the enemies of freedom to extend their influence.'[11]

Aid has created a dependency on the donors, an economic prop whose sudden removal would be catastrophic for the recipient government. Increasingly, Bangladesh must follow the advice and instructions of the World Bank and the IMF, institutions whose political make-up leads them to encourage privatization, a reduction in the role of the public sector, and increased foreign investment. After independent statehood was achieved in 1971, the new Bangladeshi government adopted a number of far-reaching radical policies – nationalization, control on foreign exchange, and limits on foreign investment. Only three years later, with food shortages and overwhelming debt plunging the country into crisis, the World Bank was called in to convene an 'Aid to Bangladesh Group', and the IMF granted further (conditional) emergency loans.

The price paid was dear: the private sector was again promoted, with investments flowing primarily to rich businesspersons who offered the greatest scope for profit. The focus of the economy was thus shifted in favour of Bangladeshi entrepreneurs who had access to credit, production resources and, increasingly, cheap labour. Exporting raw materials, particularly jute, came to assume top priority. How else could the country continue to pay for machinery and luxury goods so coveted by the powerful middle-class minority? Instead of meeting basic domestic needs such as food production, scarce resources were increasingly diverted to export-oriented activities. For example, the Second Plan (1980) allocated eight times as much to developing fertilizer factories for export, as to developing local cottage industries. While Bangladeshi farmers have the lowest fertilizer consumption in Asia, their country is well on its way to becoming a major fertilizer *exporter*. Similarly, US$40 million was allocated for the exploration of gas and oil in 1979–80. The country is a potentially rich picking ground for the big oil companies such as Shell and Total who began test drilling in 1981.

Alternatives

If existing patterns of international aid have benefited mainly relatively well-off city dwellers and landowners, to the detriment of the poor rural majority, what would be a more effective course of action? To begin with, greater stress must be placed on popular participation – involving poor communities in the design and execution of development projects, where they themselves identify needs. Bangladesh has a number of thriving indigenous organizations attempting to break the cycle of poverty. For example, Gonoshasthaya Kendra (GK), begun in 1971 by a group of young medical people, trains village health workers (mainly women) to deal with nutrition, hygiene, immunization and family planning. The area where they work now has some of the lowest infant mortality and birth rates in Bangladesh. GK has its own pharmaceutical factory, selling basic drugs up to 50 per cent cheaper than commercial imported ones.

Aid should also be directed specifically to rural agricultural development and to poor producers, particularly in famine-vulnerable areas. An interesting and unusual example of governmental aid being put to good use is the Land Reclamation Project, funded by the Dutch government. In 1985 a cyclone drove a huge wave over parts of southern Bangladesh, killing some 12,000 people. Large areas of agricultural land were flooded, areas inhabited only by the poor. This area, however, is a crucial way out of the poverty trap for some. The Land Reclamation Project has enabled people who were previously landless to farm some 4,000 acres. It has been handed over to cooperatives of previously landless peasants who have initiated training programmes for basic farming skills. Food and cash for work programmes not only provide valuable employment opportunities, but they are also important for construction initiatives designed to minimize the effects of any future cyclones. Plans for a further 60,000 acres are already well advanced.

While small successes may point the way to more general improvements in the allocation and use of aid, they do little to redress an overall picture of an era of aid that has failed the world's poor. The recognized target set by the United Nations for the quantity of aid each donor country should be contributing is 0.7 per cent of GNP. The target has, however, been reached by very few; the OECD average in 1985 was only half this figure. As we have shown, quantity is only part of the equation, but an important part, nonetheless. Private aid agencies on the whole have had a great deal more success in identifying worthwhile programmes in Bangladesh and elsewhere but their funds, and hence their impact, are extremely limited relative to those made available through bilateral and multilateral agencies. Where aid continues to be linked not to genuine development, but to the aim of sustaining political allegiance and economic dependency, it will simply reinforce precisely those power relations – international and local – that create and perpetuate hunger. Aid cannot reach the powerless when channelled through the powerful. It is not sufficient for an aid official to explain away the funding of inappropriate projects by saying, 'that is what their government asked for'. The campaign for real change in the priorities of overseas aid begins with the question, 'What are the people themselves asking for?'

4

Losing the Trade Game

> You take the earth from out of the earth
> You throw the corpses in
> One crop is as good as another
> As long as the cash comes pouring in
>
> The wheels must never stop turning
> The machine must be obeyed
> The future has got to be fueled
> And there's a price to be paid.
>
> Leon Rosselson, *Who Reaps the Profits, Who Pays the Price?*

We have seen that most developing countries are crippled by the debt crisis, face sky-high oil prices and receive little assistance. They are also subject to an 'international division of labour' that rests on the assumption that it is more beneficial for some countries in the South to produce only one or two primary crops for export, while the North produces the bulk of the world's industrial goods.

Essentially, this is a question of power relations at an international level: the poorer countries of the South export greater and greater quantities of agricultural cash-crop commodities in exchange for greater and greater quantities of vital foodstuffs from abroad. When the prices of their exports fall, and the prices of imports rise, poor countries have no control over either.

This situation did not come about overnight. Trade in commodities – raw materials, money and, even, people – as a means of extracting wealth from one country for the benefit of another, dates back to Roman times or even earlier. For our purposes, though, a useful starting date in the story of how the developing world was *incorporated* into the capitalist economy of the North, is 1492 – when

Columbus 'discovered' America. From this time onwards, the quest for commodities opened up the whole world as a trading ground, and enormous wealth settled in the hands of a few European families.

The first commodity extracted for profit from the 'New World' was sugar. Portuguese settlers in Brazil established plantations in the 1530s, and sugar became the first tropical crop to be developed specifically for the export market. Sugar plantations, investments and the use of slaves from West Africa and the Congo were to become models for later developments.

Although labour relations and conditions changed significantly over the following centuries, one vital ingredient of capitalism remained the same: profit depended on an abundance of cheap, expendable labour.

The sugar trade was dominated by the Dutch West India Company throughout the sixteenth century when the principal European trading centre was Amsterdam. The company later moved to the Carribean, where it encouraged English planters in Barbados to grow sugar, using slaves which the company initially provided. The English gradually seized the trade advantage from the Dutch and, by the mid-seventeenth century, London had become the centre for world capitalism, a position that it held for almost three centuries.

The range of products extracted from the rich soils of the South changed with price fluctuations, wars, and even the personal tastes of kings and queens. The needs of the producer countries were rarely taken into account – ownership, technology, labour and transport were all in the hands of a few companies. Whole economies were gradually geared towards, then absorbed by, a world market dominated by a handful of Northern industrial countries.

At the time of their independence, most countries of the South found themselves with little option but to continue exporting primary commodities, usually at the expense of developing their own self-sufficiency in food. It is from these raw materials that we – the industrial North – produce the final, saleable products: chocolate from cocoa, aluminium from bauxite, tyres from rubber, soap from palm or coconut oil. Any one country is often almost totally dependent on the export of just one or two commodities. Nine countries in Africa now depend on just one crop for over 70 per cent

The Colonial Mission

The real motives for colonialism, were they stated, would be altogether too uncouth, selfish or obscene. So where colonization has involved people – where it has not meant merely the appropriation and settlement of unused lands – the colonists have almost always seen themselves as the purveyors of some transcendental moral, spiritual, political or social worth. The reality has as regularly included a considerable component of pecuniary interest, real or anticipated, for important participants. Those who have questioned the myth have been lucky to be considered merely wrong; far more often they have been thought unpatriotic or traitorous.

J. K. Galbraith, *The Age of Uncertainty*

You know, long ago they used to say,'. . . the missionaries came to Africa and they had the Bible and we had the land. And then they said, "Let us pray". And when we opened our eyes, we had the Bible and they had the land!'

Archbishop Desmond Tutu

of their income; Burundi takes 90 per cent of its income from coffee; Bangladesh takes 60 per cent of its export earnings from jute products.[1]

Attempts have been made to diversify into new crops, light industry, oil or tourism. But the capital for such projects must come from existing exports; if profits are low, the countries of the South are forced to borrow from banks and governments of the North, who thereby establish a powerful lever over them. To make matters worse, competition between developing nations for a larger share of the world market means that the price of their commodities is kept low. Thus, Colombian coffee might be played off against Brazilian coffee to the detriment of both countries. In addition, tariff barriers of the developed countries discriminate against the few industrial products that come from the South.

National self-sufficiency in food is not always the solution. Control over food supply for the poor can be obtained by other means. Saudi

Arabia's recent self-sufficiency in wheat is a case in point. It was achieved only through a level of farm subsidies far beyond the means of non-OPEC countries and was, on the face of it, extremely wasteful. There are also many places in the world where the production of cash crops on marginal land is a more sensible economic strategy – for example, the planting of *acacia senegal* trees in Sudan's arid regions, where intensive food cropping would simply destroy the land. Gum Arabic from the trees is one of Sudan's prime exports.

So it is not simply a matter of choice – whether developing countries produce cash crops for export or food crops for self-sufficiency. Rather, it is a question of striking a balance between the two that benefits the poorest in those countries. But that balance is rarely struck because the interests of the poor are outweighed by national priorities or the demands of external agents – international agencies, Northern governments and transnational corporations. For each case that seems in favour of cash-cropping, we find numerous others that highlight the trap into which developing countries have been pushed. For instance, it is difficult to see how the stripping of prime forest for growing soya-beans to feed poultry eaten in Britain could benefit Brazil.

Given that the commodities produced by the South are still in demand in the North, why do the producers receive ever-decreasing returns for their goods? The answer lies, first, in the terms of trade and who fixes those terms; and, second, in the failure of the current *world* economic system to adhere to the usual rules of supply and demand.

The Road to Underdevelopment

In the three centuries following the 'discovery' of the New World, the flow of capital from Latin America, Asia and Africa to the metropolitan countries was approximately 1,000 million.[2] The drain of capital from the colonies continued right up to the end of colonial rule and, indeed, beyond. In most countries, only the export sector of the economy developed. The rest became more backward as local crafts were replaced by cheap manufactured goods from Europe and elsewhere. More and more people were employed on the plantations and the only significant investment was in export agriculture.

Western Civilization

Sheets of tin nailed to posts
driven in the ground
make up the house.

Some rags complete
the intimate landscape.

The sun slanting through cracks
welcomes the owner

After twelve hours of slave
labour.

breaking rock
shifting rock
breaking rock
shifting rock
fair weather
wet weather
breaking rock
shifting rock

Old age comes early

a mat on dark nights
is enough when he dies
gratefully
of hunger.

Agostinho Neto, First President of Angola

We can see, then, that the colonies – most countries of the South – were left with distorted economic structures; in other words, they were *underdeveloped*. Some have argued that the 'benefits' of colonialism must be accounted for – health, education and improved administration. But the facts do not bear this out. In Africa, for

Small, appropriate inputs, such as money to buy cattle and ploughs, has made all the difference to these farmers in Tigray, northern Ethiopia.
Jon Bennett/Andes Press Agency

example, only piecemeal educational services were provided. Northern Rhodesia, with an African population of 2 million, possessed only one secondary school offering higher education certificates by 1958.[3] The situation did marginally improve in some colonies as they approached independence, but only at the demand of the emerging nationalist groups whom the Europeans, in their own interest, needed to educate.

The colonial economic system provided little incentive for investment or innovation. Labour was cheap and abundant and wealth concentrated in the hands of a few landowners or mineowners. Although not all profits drained away to Europe, it was easier for the ruling classes to invest their money directly in European industry or spend it on imported manufactured goods, rather than plough it back into indigenous development.

Black Labour, White Wealth

What raised Liverpool and Manchester from provincial towns to gigantic cities?. . .Their present opulence is as really owing to the toil and suffering of the Negro as if his hands had excavated their docks and fabricated their steam-engines.

Professor Merivale, lecture at Oxford University in 1840

In pre-colonial times, Africa, like other continents, suffered from low productivity, seasonal shortfalls and occasional localized famines. On the whole, however, people were able to build up stocks in order to cope with periodic plagues like drought or locusts, especially in countries with free and equitable access to land. Except for imperial countries like Ethiopia, famine on a grand scale in Africa is largely a modern phenomenon. By the middle of the twentieth century, the neglect of the rural economy, coupled with the migrant labour system, and the enclosure of lands by the Europeans, had provoked a continental crisis.

But this was not the whole story. Once the importation of raw materials from the colonies had bolstered a rapidly expanding industry at home – as, for example, in the British textile industry, which depended so heavily on cotton from Sudan – the *domestic* market in the rich North became too small for the amount of goods being produced. Hence, overseas markets were sought – in precisely those same countries now colonized by the Europeans. The case of cotton is an illuminating example: cotton brought from Sudan went towards the production of Lancashire cloth which was then exported to India. By the middle of the nineteenth century, India was importing a quarter of all British cotton exports, and elaborate restrictions almost totally destroyed India's indigenous textile industry.

Unilever: Profits and People

Unilever is the world's biggest food and soap company. Its food labels now include Bird's Eye, Batchelors, Walls, MacFisheries, Liptons, Blue Band, Spry, Echo, John West, Stork, Krona, Oxo and Brooke Bond. It is the biggest advertiser on earth and spends more money on advertising than many governments spend on the education of their people.

Unilever began as a small soap-producing company, identified through brand names such as Lux, Vim and Pears. But, like all surviving transnationals, its expansion was both horizontal (more products) and vertical (taking control of each stage of production). Through the early part of this century, it established plantation economies in the Belgian Congo and Nigeria, forcing thousands of Africans off their land and into a state of dependency on the concession company. Starting with palm oil, it extended into production of groundnuts, cocoa, hides and skins.

Unilever's satellite company in Africa, the United Africa Company (UAC) dominated the economies of these countries in the colonial period. In post-independence years, though, it gradually pulled out, leaving the ownership of land and labour to the new governments. Very soon it was to discover cheaper sources of raw material and labour in South-East Asia and South America. Former territories in Africa were left with little choice but to continue planting more groundnuts, palm, or coconut to try to maintain revenues.

The international market for these commodities was still dominated by Unilever; the local African market could not compete. 'Corporate flexibility' – the compulsion to seek ever more profitable ground – had won the day.

The colonial era left most countries of the South in a state of dependency from which they have been slow to recover. Most of the major trends noted above are still discernible today. If one were to go into any general stores in, say, Khartoum, the 'new market' for European and American goods becomes all too apparent. The shelves are lined with imported products: scented soap replaces the more effective local scrubbing soap; refined white bread takes the place of high-fibre local bread; powdered baby milk is advertised as 'better' for your child, but causes a great many deaths from contaminated plastic bottles and unread instructions; and drugs, banned or only available through prescription in the producer-country, are sold across the counter to anyone who can afford them.

The list goes on; not all these commodities are useless or dangerous, but a great many cannot be manufactured locally. The stunted and uneven growth of local economies has seen to that. At the same time, the process of specialization – the 'international division of labour' espoused by economists of the early part of this century (and by some, still, today) – has ensured that local food production itself has declined dramatically. In the 1930s, countries of the South could still export 12 million tons of grain a year; by the early 1980s, they had to *import* nearly 80 million tons.[4]

Whose Land is it, Anyway?

Since 1985, many thousands of small landowners from Brazil's North-Eastern region have fled to the south, victims of the increasingly violent appropriation of land for large-scale cash-cropping. Intimidation and the continuing squeeze on their low income has made it impossible for these people to sustain a life of self-sufficiency in a country whose agriculture is geared almost entirely to the export market, and to the production of sugar, itself the source of alcohol fuel for the minority of Brazilians who can afford an automobile.

Paulino, a farmer from the province of Bahai, travelled thousands of miles south to find an alternative:

There is no land to work on any more, due to mechanization. We were thrown off the land we were working; the *pistoleiros* [hired gangs] came after me, threatening to kill me if I didn't leave the area. I used to grow beans, rice, sweet potato and manioc. We had comfort for the family; also some chickens and pigs. Now on my old land they grow only soya and wheat. The poor, the small people, can't work any more because only the transnationals can grow these crops. So we moved down here to look for different land. But I think there is not much hope.

The International Economic System

If international trade and economics is linked to poverty and hunger, how does the system work? Why do enormous inequalities persist between North and South when each are part of a system that purports to be 'neutral'?

Standard modern economic theory supposes that for a system to produce all the goods and services people want and need, many 'factors of production' must come into play. These include labour, energy, technological know-how, etc. – and capital. Capital is not just cash, but the accumulated means to produce – that is, trucks, lathes, tractors, steel mills or (in the case of simple agriculture) spades and hoes.

Combined with labour and other 'factors of production', capital generates goods to sell – hence, wealth. In a *capitalist* economic system, however, the one vital ingredient for producing wealth is *investment*; in other words, not manufacturing goods for immediate consumption, but generating money (financial capital) to be re-invested to produce more capital and hence – in the long term – more output. To compete in the world today, one must constantly have an eye to the rate of *growth*.

Poor countries have very little capital and low rates of saving, because such a high proportion of their wealth must be spent on consumption of basic necessities. They can only generate more capital by interacting with international trade and aid systems. About 85 per cent of capital investment in developing countries comes from their own internal savings, generated mostly by international trade.[5] More than two-thirds of this comes from agriculture. But such exports account for only a small fraction – about one-quarter – of total world trade, the great bulk of which takes place in the North. So, even though developing countries are dependent on exports for the generation of wealth and capital, their actual share in world trade is very small. The entire African

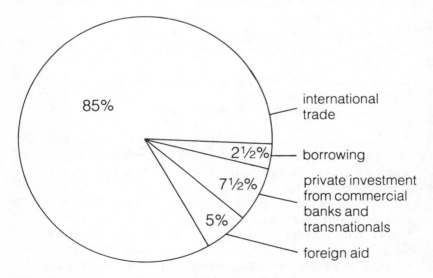

Figure 6 Sources of capital investment in developing countries
Source: World Bank, 1984

continent, for example, represents only about 4 per cent of the world's yearly imports and exports.[6]

Because income is so low in these countries, capital growth is very slow, and rarely keeps apace with population growth. Governments are having to look increasingly to external sources to keep consumption rates constant, let alone help economic growth. The remaining 15 per cent of capital investment comes from these external sources, of which there are three:

Foreign Aid By the early 1980s, about 30 per cent of external funding came from official foreign aid from the North. Most of this assistance was given to improving publicly owned capital – roads, dams, ports, etc. The pitfalls in such kinds of funding were discussed in chapter 3.

Borrowing An increasing proportion of capital investment in developing countries comes from borrowing, either privately (commercial banks) or publicly (governments or the IMF/World Bank). After the oil price increases of the early 1970s, the level of borrowing increased rapidly, from US$6.6 billion in 1970 to an unprecedented US$48.1 billion in 1981.[7] Although it has dropped slightly ($36.8 billion in 1984), the debt trap shows no sign of releasing its victims.

Private Investment About half of all external resources and finance going from the rich North to the poor South comes from private investors – primarily, commercial banks and multinationals. But ownership of this capital is partly or wholly in the hands of those investors – and, of course, profits flow back to the owners.

Although aid, investment and borrowing assume ever greater importance for the flagging economies of the South, it is still trade in basic commodities – particularly agricultural ones – upon which their wealth depends. In fact, contrary to what many people believe, the poor world feeds the rich world: food imports by the rich world still exceed exports.

Corporate Control of Food: the case of the Philippines

Any analysis of world trade cannot overlook the importance of the

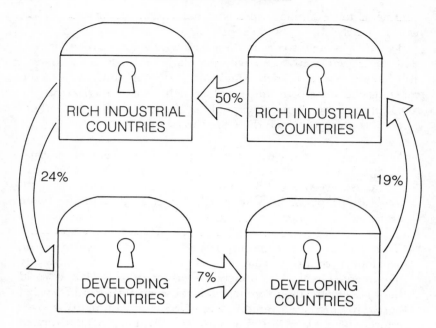

Figure 7 Trade flows as a percentage of world trade
Source: World Bank, 1984

transnationals. Their power and size are enormous. They control 40 per cent of the world's trade and up to 90 per cent of the world's commodity trade. By 1980, the world's top 30 transnationals had combined sales of US$2,700 billion, six times Britain's national income. The top 200 generate fully one-third of the Gross World Product (socialist bloc excluded).

The transnationals (TNCs) do not work alone; more often than not they depend on a country's own elites to carry forward their plans. When, for example, workers in Hawaii became unionized and demanded higher wages, TNCs moved their pineapple interests to the Philippines and Thailand, where the growth of the industry has been phenomenal. The Philippines is now the world's largest pineapple exporter. Three-quarters of its luxury produce goes to Japan, the rest to Europe or the USA. Meanwhile, the peasants cannot afford to eat what they grow.

The United Fruit Company

When the trumpet sounded, it was
all prepared on the earth,
Jehovah parcelled out the earth
to Coca-Cola, Inc., Anaconda,
Ford Motors, and other entities;
The Fruit Company, Inc.,
reserved for itself the most succulent,
the central coast of my land,
the delicate waist of America.
It rechristened its territories
as the 'Banana Republics. . .
                    Pablo Neruda, From *The Penguin Book of Socialist Verse*

Just as important as tax incentives and cheap labour, was the imposition of martial law in the Philippines in the 1970s. President Marcos, in answer to international criticism of his harsh regime, broadcast to the world in the mid-1970s his so-called land reform liberalization. Yet two-thirds of the country's agricultural land, used by the TNCs to grow export crops, was exempt from the reform. Thousands were driven from the land, while recourse to legal procedure was pointless when the country's elites apparently received 'pay-offs' to smooth things over for the TNCs.

These days, TNCs rarely own the land themselves. Rather, they retain control of trade through contracts with the big local landowners, or with the state itself. They can, thus, avoid the risk of tying up capital in land that may, if cheaper labour or crop substitutes are found elsewhere, become redundant.

The tragedy is that poor people, by definition, generate few profits. And yet, if developing countries are to promote access to food for their people, they must control new private investment so that it does not harm the interests of the poorest sectors of the society, and they must assess the merits of proposed schemes first and foremost on that basis. Palm-oil plantations were established by the Marcos regime on Mindanao Island in the Philippines, with the backing of the Commonwealth Development Corporation (CDC), allegedly on land from which peasants have been forcibly evicted. The CDC's money would have been better spent on aid projects directed at the rural poor, rather than towards export plantations.

Raw Deals

World trade and the race for foreign exchange have had an enormous impact on the poorest economies and their people. In their effort to keep up with the cost of imports, many countries are investing not in development and helping subsistence farmers to grow food, but in ploughing money into the expansion of their cash crops.

Unequal trade terms mean that these countries are getting less and less for their crops. The World Bank estimates that, if the industrialized countries cut their agricultural tariffs by half, Southern exporters would gain US$5.9 billion in extra sales of their produce.[8] But the Bank still urges more cash crop exports.

How does the world trading system work to the disadvantage of producers in the South? Let us take a closer look at two household commodities we take for granted: tea and coffee.

Tea

Tea is made from the leaves and buds of a bush that has been cultivated in China for at least 2,000 years. There are two ways of preparing the leaf; the first produces green tea, the kind drunk in China, and the second, black tea, exported mostly to the North, China itself exports only one-fifth of tea produced; likewise, India (the largest grower) exports only one-third. Although not the biggest producer, Sri Lanka exports more tea than any other country. More recently, African countries like Kenya and Tanzania have joined them in vying for export markets.

Throughout its history, the tea trade has been controlled by British companies, and Britain still imports more tea than any other country. Until about 1840, European traders had to go to the port of Canton on the coast of China for their tea. The British became addicted, but at enormous expense to the Chinese. By decree, the only authorized suppliers were powerful merchants – the 'hong' –

who provided the British East India Company with their precious leaves. To pay for it, the company smuggled opium into the country, brought from its plantations in India. As opium addiction spread in China, the Emperor stepped up his coastal patrols, finally prohibiting the entry of British ships into Canton. With the quiet blessing of Queen Victoria, British merchants, in all but name, declared war on China. The Opium War (1840–2) was one of the most one-sided wars in history; the Chinese lost not only their trade embargo and huge sums of money, but also ceded to Britain their most valuable financial and trading centre – Hong Kong.

The Chinese tea trade continued, but was soon superceded by India's. After the conquest of Bengal, the British opened huge plantations in Assam, north-east India. Labourers on five-year contracts (under the 'indenture system') were brought in to pick tea in appalling conditions. Starved off their land, they were brought under the new laws of the company, which included widespread whipping and capital punishment. But the golden age of Assam tea drew to a close in 1910 as Ceylon (now Sri Lanka) became the centre of the export trade.

Ceylon began producing tea towards the end of the last century when Sir Thomas Lipton bought 20,000 acres of cheap land for plantations. Local people refused to work for the estates, so he brought in workers from the Tamil area of South India.

India's Tamils are still working Sri Lanka's tea estates, and have been subject to much hostility from the local population (the Sinhalese) over the years. A 'land reform' programme introduced by the government in the 1970s, in which foreign-owned tea estates were nationalized, excluded Tamils, who were also deprived of their vote. It was, perhaps, inevitable that Sri Lanka was soon plunged into a bitter civil war, in which Tamil separatists took control of large areas of the country. A political solution is yet to be found. In the meantime, there are still about half a million stateless Tamils in the tea-growing areas of the country. They remain very poor, living on the brink of the poverty level set by the Sri Lankan government.

Other British companies followed Lipton's lead. Brooke Bond started producing tea in Kenya in 1925 and now owns 40,000 acres here and in India. By the 1980s, 90 per cent of the world tea market was controlled by just four companies – Brooke Bond, Lyons-Tetley, Typhoo and the Co-op.

A Tea-Picker's Day

Paramaswary is 28 years old. She makes her living as a tea-picker in Badulla, Sri Lanka. She and the other Tamil workers live in 'line' houses – long barracks near the estate, each with 24 rooms. Paramaswary, her two children, and her husband live in just two rooms. They keep coconut sleeping mats rolled in one corner, and a pile of broken firewood collected from exhausted tea bushes in the other. There is one external water tap for the 'line' of houses and a vegetable plot shared between six families.

Paramaswary works eight hours a day for an equivalent of 50 pence. Like all pieceworkers, she is expected to pick a minimum each day:

> If one of the children are ill, or I myself, I cannot pick my minimum, so I have to do more the next day. On a good day, I get extra money for overweight. My sister earns a little more than me in the processing plant, but a lot of those jobs go to the men. The *kangani* [overseer or supervisor] in the fields is also a man. He allows us to take some firewood back at nights, otherwise it costs too much in the market.
>
> Most days we eat rice, curry and papadam. Meat or dried fish is very expensive – we have it about once a fortnight. Our son is now 12 and might be given a temporary job with me on the estate next year. He will earn less than me, but it will help. But I want him to leave this place and get a good job, maybe back home in India.

The Price of a Cup of Tea

Tea is still the cheapest drink you can buy after water. The actual cost of a cup of tea is about halfpence, without milk. The breakdown is as follows:

continued

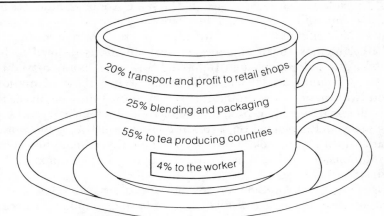

20% transport and profit to retail shops

25% blending and packaging

55% to tea producing countries

4% to the worker

Source: YTV research

Very little tea is actually packaged in the producing countries. Rather, it is sent loose in chests for auction. Most tea drunk in Britain, for example, is packeted by machine in Britain. So 25 per cent of the cost of a cup of tea goes to British companies. The four big companies control four-fifths of tea sales in Britain.

Tea is unusual amongst the products of poorer countries in that most processing is done prior to export. So the percentage of money returned to the growers (but not the workers) is higher than for most primary commodities. However, the 'real' price of tea on the world market has fallen by 25 per cent in the last ten years. 'Real' price refers to what can be bought with the money earned. Although the actual *volume* of tea on the market has increased enormously (about 60 per cent over the past 20 years), the price received by producing countries has not kept up with the sharply increasing costs for manufactured goods and other imports they buy.

Some countries, like Kenya and Zimbabwe, have established locally run cooperatives in an attempt to cut out the middlemen. They have also attempted to produce their 'own brand' teas. But foreign capital is reluctant to support this kind of initiative, so many collectives must sell their tea as 'bulk filler' to the big European companies.

The tea trade has been subject to the same economic practices as most commodities controlled by transnationals. Monopoly companies have shifted their plantations around the world according to where labour is cheap and the political climate is deemed to be 'safe'. After independence in India and Sri Lanka, many moved to Kenya, Uganda, Malawi and Tanzania. When these plantation lands were nationalized in the 1960s, they shifted their emphasis to international sales; the producer countries, although now owning the land, still depended on transnationals to sell tea on the world market for them. Brooke Bond is now the only company to retain plantations in Africa, but Northern capital still dominates the industry.

In China, tea production has developed in two ways. First, peasants are encouraged to fill quotas for local demand, but can sell any surplus on the new 'open market' of international trade. Second, because China is now vying for larger amounts of foreign capital and technology, black filler 'dust' for export is on the increase.

So the tea trade has come full circle – India undercut China, Africa competed favourably with India and Sri Lanka, and now cheap Chinese 'dust' is beginning, unwittingly, to undercut African producers. Those who lose are invariably the workers, most of whom are paid very poor wages and work in conditions of dreary monotony. Those who gain are, of course, transnational companies who completely control international trade, even if they no longer own the estates.

Coffee

After oil, coffee is the most valuable commodity in world trade. All coffee is grown in the poorer countries of the South, but about four-fifths is drunk in the richer countries of the North. Ten countries in the world depend on coffee for over half of their export earnings and the annual value of the world coffee trade is about US$15.5 billion. Aside from true addicts, coffee is an expendable item for most people in the North. When coffee prices rocketed in the mid-1970s, US consumption, for example, quickly dropped (by about 25 per cent). For the 20 million workers in the world who rely on it, however, the price paid for coffee is a matter of survival.

Coffee was first discovered in Abyssinia (now Ethiopia) over a thousand years ago. But Africa itself was a relatively late cultivator. The first commercially produced coffee came from Latin America. The French transported coffee bushes to Martinique in the eighteenth century, and Brazil became an exporter some 50 years later. Brazil is now by far the world's largest producer, accounting for one-third of all coffee grown. Indeed, nearly 80 per cent of the world's coffee trees are in Latin America.

Labouring for Luxury

Carlos Romero, one of Brazil's five million coffee workers, sets out for work with his wife and two of their five children at dawn every morning. After ten hours of back-breaking work under the scorching sun, the Romeros earn only about a penny for each pound of coffee they pick. They have no rights and no benefits, and rarely get paid until the end of the month-long harvest. They are constantly at the mercy of the landowner's seasonal needs for labour, often finding that the following month they have no work.

It is tough for us. We live in a wooden and tin house with no running water. My younger children go to the school, but the older ones must help with the work for maybe one or two months. Our wages are very low, and sometimes we feel bitter. I am told that a jar of coffee in the USA now costs $3.50 – but where does the money go?! Every year so many people want jobs here, so you have to be efficient and without sickness, otherwise you lose the chance. In the winter we move to the town for some work, if we find it – perhaps one day we will stay there.

Overall, coffee prices tend to move in cycles. There are short periods of boom, often followed by long periods of over-supply and low prices. But generally, 'real' prices have dropped steadily since the mid-1970s. Consumers tend to cut back quickly if the price goes above a certain amount; so, when there is severe frost (as in Brazil in 1975 and, to a lesser extent, in 1985) or a high level of leaf-rust disease (in Honduras in 1981), prices may first rise dramatically, but later fall to an even lower level.

In some countries, coffee production is centralized under a government organization. The washing, pulping, and bagging is done by a central agency. Thus, in Tanzania, Campaign Coffee is produced at the only instant coffee factory in East and Central Africa. A reasonably successful cooperative venture in the coffee-growing region of Bukoba, which supplies the factory, has ensured that Tanzania's farmers are better off than their neighbours in Uganda or Ethiopia. But the country's one factory still needed the assistance of multinational corporations in gaining access to markets and technology.

The Price of a Cup of Coffee

Coffee is still a fairly expensive beverage. But most of the money paid for a cup of coffee does not go to the producers. Here is the breakdown:

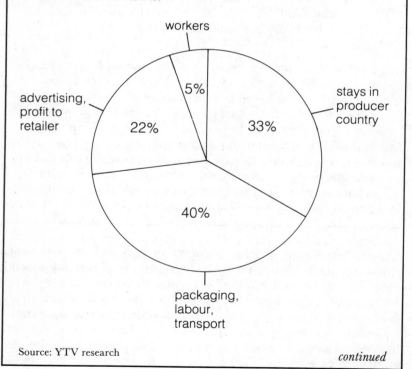

Source: YTV research

continued

Nearly 90 per cent of the coffee imported into Britain comes in as beans. The other 10 per cent is in soluble form as instant coffee, mostly from Brazil. Even so, more than half of Brazil's coffee-processing companies are foreign-owned. Major consuming countries continue to resist efforts by producers to process and manufacture their own coffee.

In other countries, individual coffee exporters buy coffee straight from the farmer or from pulperies. Much of this is then shipped to Europe or the USA and sold at a 'futures' market where contracts for delivery – and set prices – are drawn up months ahead.

Since the early 1960s, several International Coffee Agreements (ICAs) have been drawn up in an attempt to regulate quotas and smooth out changes in prices. The ICA is administered from London and attempts to find a balance between supply and demand. Because of competition between Latin American and African growers, there is unlikely to be a 'producer front' with the power to dictate its own prices. So poorer countries like Colombia, Ethiopia and Kenya, will continue to be susceptible to price fluctuations completely outside their control.

Who Throws the Dice?

The commodity markets of London and New York are closed communities, speaking a language incomprehensible to the average lay person. Yet, since the middle of the last century, they have played a crucial role in determining the price of primary commodities in the world – usually with little interest paid to the needs of the producer. In fact, it could be argued that the mechanics of the 'futures market' is the very antithesis of fair trading, for here we find capitalism operating at a rarified – even somewhat absurd – level, where real things produced by real people are abstracted beyond recognition, in what is essentially a gambling game.

The manner in which the 'futures' market works has a direct bearing on the economic fortunes of Southern developing nations dependent on selling their all-important cash crops. 'Futures' markets were developed in the 1860s in Chicago shortly after the Mid-West began large-scale grain farming. At that time, grain harvested in the autumn could not be delivered until the spring, due to the freezing over of rivers upon which all transport relied. The price of grain would be artificially high in the winter, but plummet six months later, often causing bankruptcy and extreme uncertainty for farmers.

The Chicago Board of Trade got round the problem by creating futures *contracts*. The contract would have a specified quantity, quality, time and place of delivery for the grain; and the contracts themselves became the commodity that speculators bid for. But, in fact, few contracts matured to the point at which grain would actually be delivered to the contract holder.

Futures markets now exist not just for grain, but for coffee, sugar, cocoa, etc. Most dealers on the 'floor' are young, middle-class, ambitious people whose job it is to represent a handful of powerful companies who speculate on the futures market for goods they neither produce themselves, nor even have in their possession. Basically, the idea is to buy or sell mythical goods, in the hope of accruing large profits when the price of the goods rises or falls in the future.

The 'pit' is where the actual buying and selling takes place and where, amidst a cacophony of shouting ('open outcry'), prices are determined. If it looks as though the price of a commodity – say, coffee – is going to rise because of drought in Brazil or a coup in Colombia, speculators will rush to buy stocks (contracts) for that product. Even a rumour might be sufficient. Prices artificially rise as stocks rapidly change hands. Speculators who count on higher prices are called 'bulls'.

Alternatively, some speculators might wish to sell their 'contract' before they even own it, in the hope of actually buying it later when the price is lower. Thus, it is in their interest to push the price of the stocks down after they have sold them so that when it comes to buying the actual commodity some months ahead, they will buy it at a lower price and pocket the difference. These are the 'bears'.

Only about 5 per cent of commodity transactions on these markets relate to actual delivery of goods! How, then, do the activities of the 'bulls' and 'bears' affect the economies of the developing countries?

The answer, simply, is that the rules of the game are fixed in favour of the speculators, not the producers. Merchants (or nations) dealing in *real* commodities can only insure themselves against price changes by 'hedging' their risks and 'locking in' a price for their goods over a *short* period of time. They are not protected against long-term general falls in prices. As we have seen, however, the speculators are protected(unless, of course, they guess wrong); but if the price of coffee that flashes on the electronic board today is 10 per cent less than it was last year, there is little the Brazilian government can do about it.

In summary, then, the only way poorer countries could achieve equal footing in the current world order is by taking control of the produce on the ground *and* the sale of that produce. It is worth remembering that Northern speculators gamble not only with the wealth of nations, but also with the lives of powerless farmers within those nations.

Agriculture: the Road to Salvation?

Nearly three-quarters of the population of the developing world are farmers, but government policies in most of these countries discriminate heavily against farming. By contrast, in the industrial North agriculture is universally protected and subsidized – yet only 9 per cent of the labour force works on the land.

Such contradictions have moved to the centre of world attention in recent years, particularly in the wake of Africa's famine. The imbalance in the system costs the world economy in the region of US$40 billion a year, in storage costs and subsidies.[9] While malnutrition remains endemic in the South, food stocks big enough to feed the whole of Africa five times over pile up in European and US silos.

The EEC and USA governments continue to pay their farmers to leave wheat fields fallow whilst imposing trade restrictions and tariffs on food products from the developing world. It is a sad comment on the state of global economics that Northern countries have successfully protected their farmers from the effects of tumbling world prices (and, indeed, competition from abroad), while the South has plunged into further recession. The cost in lost commodity exports for the South between 1980 and 1984 was US$38 billion.[10]

No fundamental change to these huge disparities in the world economic system is in sight. The EEC, for example, has a 1987 budget of £24.8 billion. The Common Agricultural Policy (CAP) – part of whose responsibility is to buy and store food in those

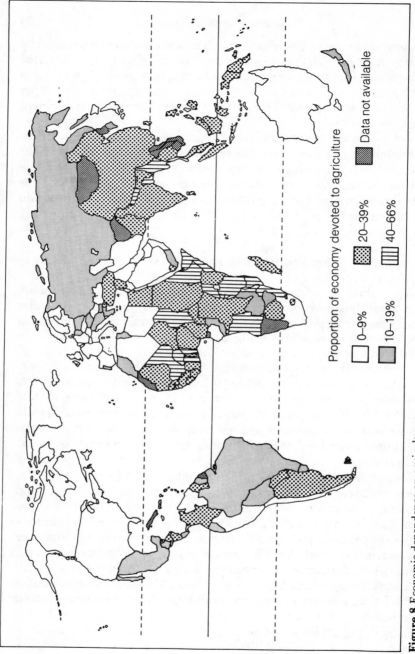

Figure 8 Economic dependence on agriculture
Source: World Bank, 1984

Proportion of economy devoted to agriculture

- 0–9%
- 10–19%
- 20–39%
- 40–66%
- Data not available

notorious silos where it either rots or is burnt – accounts for a full 64 per cent of this. By contrast, the amount allocated to development and food aid to the poorer South has dropped – to only 3 per cent of the budget.

Continuing imbalance in the terms of trade for the South hinges not only on the price of Southern export commodities, but on the level of 'protectionism' in the North – the imposition of trade barriers set up to 'protect' home produce. Traditionally, this has occurred through the use of three measures:

Tariffs – import taxes on goods from other countries, designed to make foreign goods more expensive and thus make the price of domestic goods more favourable;

Quotas – limits on the amount of foreign goods that can be imported;

Subsidies – allowances (from central government) to domestic producers that enable them to offer their goods at a cheaper rate on the world market.

The myth that the 'the market' will feed all is clearly exposed. Northern farmers are subsidized so as to be able to compete with Southern farmers whose governments *cannot* afford to subsidize them. Meanwhile, those poorer farmers are discriminated against twice over: heavily taxed by their own governments, they are then told they cannot sell their produce in Northern industrial markets. Why? Because the price isn't right, and quotas are already filled by Northern farmers.

Since 1948, there has been a series of agreed limits on international trade barriers set up through the General Agreement on Tariffs and Trade (GATT). But, until 1979, this agreement applied only to manufactured goods. The main beneficiaries were those Southern countries that managed to break into world markets through the intermediary of transnationals importing the necessary technology – countries like Hong Kong, Singapore, South Korea and Taiwan. But it was quite meaningless to the poorer developing countries.

A New International Economic Order?

An alternative approach championed by nations of the South was the United Nations Conference on Trade and Development (UNCTAD). Set up in 1964, UNCTAD can only make recommendations, but it has already been a 'test bed' for new ideas on how the world economy should be adjusted. A key element in UNCTAD discussions is the need for an expansion in manufactured goods in the South, which would entail a new stage of industrialization and a break from dependency on Northern products. To achieve this, however, the North must open its markets to higher-priced raw materials from the South, which will then be able to ensure greater capital expansion.

The lifting of trade barriers may be one step towards a more equitable system, but 'free trade' would still tend to favour stronger competitors. In order to establish an environment that supports development, some form of positive 'protection' must be given to poorer countries.

Negotiations between rich and poor countries on the so-called 'New International Economic Order' (NIEO) have so far produced few results. This is hardly surprising. Apart from OPEC countries since 1973, the developing world has yet to gain the *power* to force these kinds of demands on the North.

There are still some unpalatable truths to come to terms with. If the promotion of manufactured goods is the road to prosperity, this could well be at the expense of the mass of people in the South. Because of the need to compete with advanced countries, labour would have to be kept cheap. In addition, the strategy seems to depend on increasing imports of technically advanced equipment, and this suggests an even greater role for transnationals. Thus, the process of dependency may be cemented.

That is not all. Cheap labour, declining living standards of the urban masses, plus the dominant position of transnationals, could well encourage political repression – in particular, the destruction of trade union rights. In countries vying for the attentions of the transnationals, this is precisely what has happened already – in Brazil, Singapore, Chile and the Philippines (until the collapse of the Marcos regime in 1986). To date, the road to self-sustaining capitalist development in the South has been strewn with the victims of repressive regimes.

5

Brazil: Miracle or Mirage?

Land must be freed in order to free the human being.

Latin American peasant saying

In Brazilian folklore, it is said that at the time of the creation the angels stood back in amazement at the favours God had lavished on the country. They asked how such gifts could be justified, to which God replied, 'Just wait and see the problems I am going to give you!'

Brazil is the fifth largest country in the world and the largest in South America, constituting almost half the land area of the continent. Twenty years ago, Brazil embarked upon an 'economic miracle' – with a spectacular growth rate that put the country amongst the ten richest in the world. Huge hydroelectric power stations, massive office blocks and expensive paved roads were the hallmarks of prosperity, a leap into the modern, industrial, twentieth century.

But, behind the skyscapers and business centres, behind the Macdonald fast food shops and Japanese car factories, lives a Brazil that is chaotic, violent, very poor, undernourished and sick. Not just a few who have fallen behind, but 50 million people who live in extreme poverty. At least one-third of the population is malnourished, and 90 children per thousand die in the first 12 months, most of them from hunger.[1] These are the victims of Brazil's 'growth' – ordinary people who stand in the way of the march of progress.

Ordinary people, like 'Maria Lorca' and her husband, 'Paolo' who for 32 years have farmed their own plot of land near Rio Formosa. Though small, the land is lavishly planted with coconut trees, manioc, pineapple, and jak fruit. An idyllic setting? Hardly, for the 'Lorcas'' farm is surrounded on all sides by tall sugar cane as far

Figure 9 Brazil

as the eye can see – a massive privately owned scheme, and a symbol of Brazil's increasing consumption of sugar-based alcohol for cars. One evening, a gang hired by the plantation owners came, brandishing shotguns. They ripped up the new trees planted by the 'Lorca' family and made it quite clear that they also wanted their land, the last smallholding left in the area. Without government protection, the 'Lorcas' have come to accept that their days on the farm are numbered.

Like many thousands before them, 'Maria' and 'Paolo' will

probably find their way to the *favelas* – the shanty-towns/slums put up by people on the outskirts of every major town in Brazil. Exchanging rural poverty for urban squalor, they might, if lucky, find menial labouring jobs in one of the big modern factories. Or they could end up as casual labourers – coffee-pickers, stone breakers and weeders known locally as the *boias frias*, or cold-food people, as they never have a hot midday meal. These are Brazil's 'untouchables', doing tedious, dirty and unhealthy work for very low wages. And their numbers are growing.

Why did Brazil's economic growth bypass the majority of the population – the poor? The answer lies in who defines 'development', and who benefits from the spoils of capitalist enrichment. Brazil is certainly 'developed' in one sense; it has its own industries, and processes its own cash crops – it even has its own nuclear power stations and exports sophisticated weapons systems. But the old refrain that the 'rich get richer and the poor, poorer' might have been invented for Brazil. Wealth *disparity* is what keeps so many thousands there on the list of the world's hungry.

In our search for the inequalities that lie behind world hunger, we soon become aware that social status – where one belongs in the class system – can make an enormous difference to one's chance of survival. There is a margin of 19 years between the life expectancies of the highest and lowest income groups in Brazil. A general's wages equal that of about 200 ordinary workers. On a visit to Europe in 1984, Cardinal Dom Lorscheider from North-East Brazil said, 'We can no longer talk about development and underdevelopment in Brazil, we must talk about liberation and oppression.'[2] It is a measure, perhaps, of the increasing gap between rich and poor that even moderates within the Catholic Church have taken up the cry of the disposssed with such passion.

Brazil's rapid rise to national prosperity in the 1970s, leaving a trail of human adversity in its wake, was not a problem of 'too much, too soon'. Rather, it was a classic example of a development strategy imposed from 'above' – the passing of wealth from one set of elites to another, each assuring themselves of the 'trickle-down' effect that the Brazilian people would sooner or later enjoy.

But very little wealth passed into the hands of the poor. Out of Brazil's total population of 135 million, nearly 50 million people (10 million families) are landless peasants, victims of the growing concentration of land, the process by which rural estates become the property of a handful of rich landowners and agribusiness corporations. This 'rationalization' of agriculture did not take long. Although Brazil has always been known for its huge landownings, mechanization and even greater concentration of holdings has occurred since the late 1970s, on the heels of the 'economic miracle'.

Rhetoric and Reality: the Boom Years

A useful starting point in our story would be 1964 when, with the assistance of the USA, a military coup overthrew President Goulart's short-lived government. From that time onwards, the new military government ushered in a process of economic expansion, particularly in industry. By the end of the 1960s, annual industrial growth rates of 10 per cent were being recorded, unprecedented in the developing world.

At the same time, Brazil opened its doors to uncontrolled foreign investment, especially from the USA. The powerful transnationals moved in, promoting a model of development that attempted to reproduce the patterns of modernization seen in the richer Northern countries. But Brazil's growth was initially in one direction only, towards the production of consumable goods – automobiles, electrical goods and the like. In other words, it served a limited market, perhaps only 10 per cent of the population could afford these new luxuries.

A modern industrial sector was simply grafted on to the country at the behest of government agents faithful to this 'modernization' model. From the mid-1960s, the whole *structure* of Brazilian society was moulded by transnational companies and their executives, whether foreign or Brazilian. Large sums of money fell into the pockets of a few; for millions more, however, the quality of life dramatically deteriorated.

How was Brazil able to attract foreign capital and multinational investment, so central to the government's modernization blueprint? The answer lay in the 'triple bribe', tried and tested in so many countries of the world – low taxes, repressive labour laws and low wages, in return for financing economic growth. Thus, the national labour force was almost totally immobilized, unable to voice dissent through the unions or on the streets. Labour leaders were imprisoned and increasingly repressive laws kept strikes to a minimum.

The *Favelados*

2.5 million people live in the shanty-towns on the outskirts of Sao Paulo, and new *favelas* are springing up all the time. They are formed by people squatting on land that is not theirs and building wooden shacks wherever there are a few square feet to spare. Often, there is no access for refuse trucks and sanitation is appalling. Local councils may occasionally provide electricity and water for those who pay the small rental. Conditions are cramped, but few can afford to move to city flats where rents are extremely high.

The people who live in these shanty-towns, the so-called *favelados*, are mostly victims of land battles, mechanization and the illusive dream of an affluent life in the city. Each family tells a story of perpetually moving around the country in search of land or work. When they settle on the outskirts of a city such as Sao Paulo the men find, at best, work as factory hands or cane cutters, but wages are insufficient for the whole family. Often children as young as 12 will begin full-time work whilst transferring to state-run 'night schools'.

Rocio lives with her husband and two children in a wooden *favela* perched high on the hillside near Sao Paulo. Three years ago they came here in search of occasional work, but more often than not depending on state hand-outs.

> We bought this house with difficulty. Before, we were living under bridges. We paid CRS200,000 [about US$20] for this, but it has a lot to be done. We have to get material to replace the roof. We don't have electricity, we have nothing. . .but it is better than being on the street. My husband cuts cane. He earns very little, so we eat beans, flour, pasta, but no meat, nor coffee, just tea. Sometimes we are without money on a Thursday or Friday, so we don't have food for the weekend. . .This is my young girl. She is sick, her skin is always itching, and she gets nervous.

Throughout the 1960s and 1970s, peasant leagues were outlawed, freedom of the press was curtailed and Brazil added another superlative to its list of achievements: it became the first South American country to set up a regime based on the Doctrine of National Security. Ostensibly to protect democratic institutions against 'communist' take-over, the doctrine ensured tight control over Congress and the judiciary. Political opposition was curbed in the name of 'national security'; and violations of human rights became an everyday occurrence.

The compression of wages during those years is perhaps most starkly demonstrated by events in Sao Paulo. The infant mortality rate in the city during the 'miracle' decade rose by 45 per cent. As inflation soared, people were obliged to work longer hours to compensate for the reduced purchasing power of their wages. Many were pushed to the periphery of the city by the rise in property values, and deprived of a minimum standard of nutrition, sanitation, and health care for their families.

US investments in Brazil quadrupled from 1964 to 1970, as the country became an important ally in the so-called US 'backyard'. Transnationals continued to enjoy high profit margins, and this allowed them to remit far greater amounts of money abroad, and to increase savings for new investments. Initially, they put their money into Brazil's expanding heavy industry. Endowed with considerable mineral wealth, the country now mines its own ores, processes the metal with its own machinery and sells the finished products at home and abroad.

It was at this time that Brazil earned its reputation as the country of the car. The largest factory in Latin America is Volkswagen in Sao Paulo. Here people queue to be employed at wages less than a quarter of those paid to their counterparts in Europe. Since the mid-1970s, the face of modernity has also shown a more sinister side: some companies are reported to have had security cells where those late for work, those suspected of being in a worker's organization, or the like, could be locked up for hours. Working conditions, also, were poor; today, roughly 30 per cent of the work-force still suffer

---

Favelas in Recife – millions live here on the margins of Brazil's 'economic miracle'.
J. C. Gadmer/CIRIC

industrial accidents each year because employers are not compelled
to enforce safety legislation.[3]

Cap Intensive High technology, though generating greater productivity, also
creates unemployment as machines do the work of people. New
industries in the towns and in agriculture have destroyed badly
needed jobs and pushed increasing numbers on to the streets. There
are now at least 12 million underemployed people in Brazil.

Selling it on the Box

Brazil is considered among the top five advertising markets in
the world – about 60 per cent of all (transnational) advertising
expenditures are channelled through television. One network –
Globo – is the fifth largest in the world. Globo has developed a
very sophisticated TV sales-technique called merchandising. It
sells advertising spots within its leading soap operas – actually
as part of the story. For example, in the soap *Rocky Santero*, a
leading actor will enter a shop and ask for a particular brand of
biscuit. The audience will not be aware that General Foods has,
in fact, 'bought' that space so that people identify the biscuit
with their favourite character. *Rocky Santero* is beamed into even
the most remote rural villages – but who can afford to buy the
biscuits?

The Miracle Turns Sour

From 1973 onwards, governments of the more 'dynamic' developing
nations, particularly those in Latin America, had a further source of
finance to turn to: the private commercial banks. Huge sums of
'cheap' money were quickly made available. As their ledgers
overspilled with petro-dollars from the newly rich OPEC countries,
the banks began to look for 'sink-holes' in the South (see chapter 4).
In 1970, US$7.73 billion was lent to developing countries. By 1981,
loans had risen to US$25 billion – the largest share going to Brazil
and Mexico.[4]

For Brazil, the 'carrot' was very low interest rates, as little as
3.5–4.5 per cent per annum. Favourable circumstances in the 1970s
meant that there was little reason to fear that the country would not

repay its accumulating debt. After all, so the argument ran, a country with maturing heavy industry, rich natural resources, and an expanding export market for cash crops, would surely sustain growth for many years to come.

This optimism was short-lived. Several factors were not accounted for. First, monetarist policies of Northern nations plus the growing US budget deficit caused interest rates to soar from 4 per cent to more than 18 per cent in 1981 (it has since dropped to about 12 per cent). Second, world recession reduced the demand for Brazil's exports, causing commodity prices to plummet.

Increasing Poverty

The type of capitalism Brazil chose to follow came to be frustrating for capitalists themselves, because it created social instability. The model followed by the business community was one of intensive investments in certain sectors – taking into account only 15–20 per cent of the population as a worthwhile market, and marginalising the rest. The problem for the IMF in the 1980s has been how to re-establish an economic balance in the country without depressing even further the condition of the poor.

How could they do this without causing social disruption? I think they didn't think twice about it. They simply said, well let's use the traditional model to overcome the crisis. The result has been three years of increasing poverty. The masses die of starvation. There was never a period in Brazilian history as bad as this.

Marcos Arruda, Brazilian economist, 1986

Ironically, the increase in the price of oil itself dealt a severe blow to Brazil's 'miracle'. The economy had depended on cheap oil to transport raw materials, agricultural and manufactured goods around the vast country. In spite of the increase in oil prices, grandiose development plans went ahead – not least the building of huge prestige projects such as the Tucuriu hydroelectric dam in the Amazonian basin.

By the 1980s, Brazil's whole economic system had to be reshaped in response to the increasing demand for dollar repayments on loans made 10 years previously. Today, the country faces a foreign debt of US$103 billion. Servicing that debt means pushing for more exports; in other words, pursuing the 'growth before distribution' model of development. The poor majority – even the middle classes – are paying the price.

Brazil today exemplifies uneven development writ large: it has the biggest factory, and the biggest slums in South America; it also has the largest foreign debt of any developing nation in the world and, in 1981–3, experienced negative rates of growth. Although by 1986 the economy was growing again (at a slow rate of 8 per cent), the slump has left permanent scars.

The Riches of the Land

Brazil is the fifth largest country in the world, covering an area of 3.3 million square miles. It has borders with eight out of the other ten South American countries and has thousands of miles of coastline. Rich in natural resources, the country could potentially provide more than enough land for all, yet the struggle over land remains at the centre of the country's political upheavals.

Brazil exports coffee, soya beans, beef, orange juice and other agricultural products to earn foreign exchange. Millions more acres have been taken over for sugar production – most of it not for export, but for conversion into fuel for cars to limit the imports of petrol. Promotion of the commercial agricultural sector at the expense of subsistence farming has greatly encouraged urbanization and an increasing reliance on food imports. In 1960, Brazil was producing excess food, which was exported to neighbouring countries. Today, however, many basic foods such as rice and beans are imported. Cereal imports in 1985 reached 5.4 million tons.[5]

There has been an unprecedented exodus to the cities since the mid-1960s. The number of people living solely off the land has halved; the rural population now constitutes only 30 per cent of Brazil's 135 million people. This massive movement of people has gone hand in hand with commercial agricultural growth, whereby mechanized farms are owned by fewer and fewer landowners. The shift has been most marked in the fertile southern region, but the same economic policies and priorities have affected the entire country.

By the mid-1970s, it became clear that a highly sophisticated agricultural sector could provide valuable dollars for Brazil's waning economy. There was also, potentially, a huge domestic market for the tractors and farm machinery being produced in the cities. The race for high yields was on. Tax concessions were given to encourage mechanization, plus a guaranteed minimum price for cash crops such as soya beans. In addition, the government began to provide generous loans – the state-owned Banco do Brasil is reportedly the largest agricultural lender in the capitalist world.[6]

Just how this affected people and environment differed in each of Brazil's three main areas: the Amazon basin, the North-East 'Drought Polygon',[7] and the fertile Central and Southern regions.

The Amazon Basin

By far the largest of the three regions is Amazonia, where one-third of the world's tropical rain-forests can be found. Teeming with exotic insects and birds, it is populated by rapidly depleting tribes of Indians who retain their traditional life-styles against pressure from land clearance and cultivation. The rain-forests are dissected by the mighty Amazon river, longer than the distance between Liverpool and New York. It empties 7.5 million gallons of water into the sea every second and its basin is as large as the USA.

Sadly, the quest for land and wood is fast destroying the forest, and environmentalists world-wide are concerned for the earth's oxygen supply and effect on the planet's climate. 40 per cent of the world's tropical forests have been cleared over the last 20 years.

Apart from a brief period of rubber exploitation around the time of the First World War, this vast region was ignored until the 1960s. Only then, with the opening of the Belem–Brasilia highway, was it rudely brought into the twentieth century. The natural wealth of the area was suddenly discovered: first hardwoods, especially mahogany, were cut down in huge quantities; then lands for grazing were cleared; and, finally, gold and other minerals were exploited, mostly by transnational companies.

Bishop Patrick Hanrahan from the Diocese of Conceicao do Araguaia in the Amazon takes up the story:

> Inevitably, this wealth attracted all sorts: the greedy, the
> adventurers, the speculators, the 'prudent' businessmen who

wanted at once a safe investment and Government tax incentives; the farmers who wanted to found here a permanent home for themselves and their families; the vast number of illiterate peasants who, fleeing the misery and hunger of the North-East, flock here with their wives and many children, their hearts full of hope in this green land of promise, and confident of the government commitment to give 'this land without people to people without land'. The Diocese of Conceicao itself is nearly the size of the Republic of Ireland, yet there is no land for the poor, in spite of the existence in the Statute Books – though rarely enforced – of Federal agrarian reform laws of more than sixteen years' standing. Here is one of the roots of the violence, the killings, the oppression, that plague the region.[8]

A third of the entire area occupied by 77 Indian reserves in the greater Amazon basin has been requisitioned by mining companies. Some 40 per cent of these companies are transnationals. The total prospecting rights already granted cover an area of 17 million hectares out of the 52 million occupied by the Indian reserves. Today, only 200,000 Indians remain from an estimated 7 million who occupied this land before the turn of the century. The human impact of this 'discovery' of wealth has been immense. Successive Brazilian governments have been guilty of corruption, mismanagement and even genocidal attacks on Amazonian Indians, many of whom are left with little alternative but to move to the slums of industrial cities.[9]

The mining companies' rush to the Amazon was sparked by the chance discovery of the giant Carajas iron ore mining field; but the main interest today is in gold and the carving of a new export corridor to the northern ports. The trans-Amazonia highway was built to facilitate easier access to the coast, particularly for those involved in mining and cattle ranching. Communities sprang up alongside the road in the early days in the hope of finding land of their own, but the Amazonian soil has been found lacking. In only a few years, new land is abandoned. Many people have subsequently left and the road is in a state of disrepair.

Much-vaunted symbols of progress in the region are the Tucurui hydroelectric dam and the nearby Belem and Sao Luis aluminium plants, not far from the mouth of the Amazon. Yet, pollution and degradation of the environment go hand in hand with this development geared towards the cities and, even there, only a small minority will benefit. The Sao Luis aluminium plant required the expulsion of 20,000 families from their land with little compensation and toxic gases now spill from the plant, endangering plant and fish life upon which the local population has depended for centuries.

The North-East 'Drought Polygon'

Brazil's second region is the North-East plateau, the dry semi-desert that stretches from the Amazon basin almost to the Atlantic coast. Seven years of drought has decimated an already sparse population that tries to scratch a living from the land, growing cassava and beans and rearing livestock. More recently, 2.5 million out of the estimated 24 million people living in the critically affected areas have been employed on the official public-work schemes to combat drought. These schemes – the Emergency Work Fronts – pay about £8 a month, a wage that bears no relation to Brazil's soaring inflation. More ominously, the long-term benefits of these irrigation projects will go to the rich landowners rather than to the poor.

About 70 per cent of the regions's population of 35 million were affected in some way by drought, and official 1985 figures put the number of those suffering directly from hunger and thirst at 15 million.[10] Although the drought ended in late 1985, the repercussions have been far-reaching as hundreds of thousands of *flagelados da seca* (drought refugees) migrated to the coastal region to swell the shanty towns.

In the sixteenth century, the Portuguese planted sugar along the coastal belt east of the *zona da seca* (drought region), bringing slaves from Africa to cut the cane. Since then, settlement and cropping patterns have been determined not by local needs, but by the demands of the international market. Land tenure systems have been essentially feudal – subsistence farming has been embedded within the commercial *latifundia* structure; that is, large cash-crop estates where landowners concede grazing rights to small farmers in return for labour. The system permits a remarkable imbalance of wealth: 9 per cent of landowners possess nearly 82 per cent of the land in the North East.

These feudal patterns are now changing. Rural workers are today encouraged and pressurized to leave their small plots for the *favelas*,

Sao Paulo Widow

Margarida Nascimento, a 37-year old mother of five –
'There were seven, but two of them died' – gets up at 3.00 a.m.,
heats up two cups of beans and coffee and prepares a
porridge of manioc flour for the children. All the children
sleep in the same room as the open fire.

Margarida is a 'Sao Paulo widow'; her husband, a
drought victim, migrated to the south in search of work –
and has not been seen since.

The woman maintains the family alone and works on an
Emergency Work Front 9 kilometres away. She locks all
the young children in the house for the day. *'I leave them in
God's hands. There is no other way'*, she says.

Margarida walks for two hours to be at the Front by 6.00
a.m. If she's not there, she loses two days' pay as
punishment. At the Front she spends four hours heaving
rocks on a dam-fortification scheme. She works for four
days a week. At the end of the month she takes home the
equivalent of £8.

'When I leave home, I have a bit of coffee with manioc
flour. That's all. Hunger pangs begin by about 10.00 a.m.,
but you have to put up with them. The ones who can't just
collapse. I've seen lots of women collapse onto the rocks.
We earn next to nothing, but the Front is the only thing
between us and death.'

Brazilian national newspaper, 14 February 1984, translated by Oxfam

company compounds or other homes. Concentration of land itself
has contributed to the social disruption caused by drought. From
1964 to 1970, the average size of smallholdings declined by 40 per
cent (from 5.55 to 3.63 hectares).[11] With such a small amount of
land from which to scrape a living, it took only a slight fall in
production to push many over the brink. They sold their livestock
and tools and moved to the towns. Thus, the drought itself further
shifted the balance in favour of capital-intensive agribusiness in the
North East.

Central and Southern Regions

Towards the end of the 1970s, Brazilian agriculture benefited from roughly US$18 billion in credit and loans at very favourable rates. The flood of money on the international market, plus the priorities of the government, ensured that there were large profits to be made from the land, particularly in the richer Central and Southern regions. Brazil was soon transformed into one of the richest agricultural nations in the Southern hemisphere.

There is a law on the Brazilian statute books that conveys right of tenure on anyone who has lived upon and cultivated a piece of public land for a year and a day. In Brazil today, the law is not only rarely implemented, but openly flouted, as more and more peasant families are forcibly evicted from their land to make way for large sugar, cocoa, soya bean or coffee schemes. As the number of those solely dependent on subsistence farming has decreased, the number of rural wage labourers has increased dramatically. In Sao Paulo, for example, one of the southern states where Brazil's 'agricultural miracle' was centred, the number of agricultural day-workers swelled by almost 175,000 in the last half of the 1960s to reach 350,000 by 1980.[12]

There is an interesting comparison between what is now happening in Amazonia and what happened in southern areas such as Parana in the 1950s. Forests were cut down and farmers began to establish successful smallholdings, only to be replaced very quickly by big mechanized farms. Already the signs are that intensive cultivation and lack of care for the land is having serious consequences; some land has been abandoned altogether because of erosion; other land is now only suitable for cattle grazing.

By the mid-1980s, the number of agricultural workers in Central and Southern regions had declined from 48 per cent of the national work-force in 1965 to less than 30 per cent by 1986. [13] Yet, still, about 10 million workers and their families are landless agricultural workers whose salaries bear no relation to inflated prices in the cities where they live.

Meanwhile, Brazil is moving further away from self-sufficency in basic foodstuffs. International loans have helped consolidate the growth of the commercial farming sector – for example, the World Bank's recent pledge of US$202 million to provide agricultural

In Their Own Words

It might seem incredible, but the sugar cane cutter during the harvest gets more than the minimum wage of a factory worker. They say some are unemployed, but I don't believe it, because there is always a lack of workers during the harvest. I think that the cane worker can live reasonably well despite what the political campaigners say.

Farmowner, North-East Brazil, 1986

When he comes back home from work with some money I even cry. I look at the situation with my daughters – no shoes, hungry, and nobody to help us. I have to do something, so I go fishing with my husband, and try to get something, but life is really difficult. Sometimes I feel like getting a gun and going out stealing things. The salary does not go up, and he comes homes very tired.

Wife of a cane cutter, North-East Brazil, 1986

credit – but little of this will find its way to the domestic food producers. Almost all of it will go to the production of export crops.

Debt and Political Stability

In common with most other developing countries, Brazil faces a two-fold attack on the economy. First, there is a considerable fall in the real value of her exports – hence the need to produce even greater amounts of soya beans, cocoa, cashew-nuts, etc. Second, is the rise in interest rates on debts accumulated in the 1970s. The former has exacerbated problems of land and productivity; the latter has given Brazil the dubious honour of having the world's second biggest overdraft (after the USA). Debt rescheduling in 1984 offset at least part of this demand but, still, a full 27 per cent of Brazil's export earnings go towards interest payments on money borrowed in the 1970s.[14] Impatience is mounting; Brazil's US$103 billion debt has become almost a *cause célèbre*, inviting increasing obduracy. The country's Finance Minister, Dilson Funaro, recently stated quite bluntly: 'We will only pay what we can. If a creditor does not agree, he can send back the cheque.'

The usual response to this has been as familiar as it is unwelcome. To deal with Brazil's enormous national debt, the International Monetary Fund (IMF) has imposed strict austerity measures. These include a reduction in social expenditure, wage control and a rise in the price of basic foodstuffs – measures that hit the poorest sectors of Brazilian society. Inevitably, urban unrest has followed quick on the heels of such 'adjustment' packages. By 1986 the Brazilian government was becoming less patient with its creditors, declaring that it would increase social expenditure by 51 per cent and refuse to uphold the stringent terms laid down by the IMF.

One of the outstanding features of the Brazilian industrial scene of late has been the workers' widespread use of the strike weapon. 1979 saw a wave of strikes affecting 3 million workers in 15 out of 22 states in Brazil. In 1980, a new political party, the Workers' Party (PT), united different sectors of the working population – trade unionists, Christian communities and, increasingly, rural farmworkers. In response, the government prepared for an end to military rule with a programme of reforms known as *abertura* (the 'opening up' of political participation).

Abertura included the lifting of direct censorship, amnesty to certain political prisoners and exiles, and the legalization of opposition parties. It ended with presidential elections in 1985 and the lifting of military rule when President Tancredo Neves was elected(succeeded at his death by Jose Sarney). This was generally regarded as signalling a return to democracy, although the President was not elected by direct franchise.

In the meantime, the security of the Western banking system depends on Latin America as a whole continuing to meet its debt repayments; so, for most countries, further loans are lined up, in spite of the fact that as much as 30 per cent is said to be lost through corruption, mismanagement, and capital flight. While congresspersons in Brasilia enjoy lakeside mansions, the country's poor eke out a meagre existence where a few pence added on to the price of bread can mean the difference between life and death.

The Market Place: Names that Count

In the plush designer office of the young general manager of

Coca-Cola hangs a framed map of South America emblazoned with the Coca-Cola motif and the words: 'Brazil: largest operation in the Southern hemisphere'. Marcos Magalhaes is proud of this achievement. He puts it down to a good product and what he calls the right 'company culture': 'Coca-Cola learns to live with the local economy, local people and local laws. We have a strict code of ethics.' And he adds jokingly, 'We are more Christian than Christ.'

Coca-Cola's Brazilian operation is huge: 70 bottling plants, with half a million outlets, even though only about one-third of the population can afford to buy Coke. The company has captured an estimated 50 per cent of the soft drinks market with their four most popular brands – Coke, Fanta Orange, Sprite, and Guaraná Taï. The displacement of local drinks by the big companies is, in part, due to effective marketing, television advertising in particular. 'Coke is it!', a product that boasts 'availability, affordability and acceptability'.

But bottled soft drinks are sometimes less nutritious than traditional drinks. Fanta Orange, for example, in spite of its name contains only about 10 per cent orange juice, and that percentage was only achieved after recent legislation. Yet Brazil is the world's largest exporter of orange juice. Most is sold to the USA who put it on the shelves under the names Snow-Crop and Minute Maid. Brazilian consumption of oranges remains relatively low; and health statistics show that many poorer families suffer vitamin-C deficiency.

Guaraná Taï is Coca-Cola's answer to a popular local drink made by a process of pasteurization from the guaraná fruit grown by small farmers in the Amazon region. There is a difference, though: Coke's equivalent is almost completely artificial, using concentrates with gas and water added. Tough advertising strategy has influenced the choices available to the consumer and, at the end of the day, it is either the farmers or the consumers themselves who lose. Ironically, it seems that <u>Coca-Cola are in favour of a trickle down of wealth in Brazil</u>; as Marcos Magalhaes explains, 'At the moment the retail price is fixed by the government as part of its inflationary controls. Even so, we'd like to see more people able to afford Coke.'

The Brazilian market is a pyramid, with about 8–10 million people at the top who can afford sophisticated Western tastes. Transnationals in the food business aim their products at this group.

Coffee-picking in Brazil – cash crops for a collapsing economy.
Christian Aid

Some, like Nestlé, specialize in processed foods. But fast foods are now taking off, with Macdonalds dominating the high street. Many companies pulled out during the recession of the early 1980s, but many have an eye on long-term prospects. The processed food market in the USA has a steady 2 per cent growth rate; in Brazil it is 8 per cent. The food merchants are biding their time.

Soya Beans: the New Export Crop

After centuries as an exporter primarily of tropical commodities – bananas, sugar and coffee – Latin America is now altering its role in the international division of labour. Basically, the change is rooted in the advance of capitalism: as the productive capacity of these countries develops, the range of commodities they can produce for the world market widens.

This is illustrated by the growth of soya production in Brazil. Until the early 1970s, the USA was practically the world's only exporter of soya beans. But the tide began to change. Using mechanized farming equipment and moving on to some old coffee-producing lands, Brazil's entrepreneurs quickly challenged that monopoly. Today, much of Japan's and Western Europe's supply of soya products (including oil) come from Brazil.

Rich Brazilian landowners exploit their work-force whilst reaping large profits from intensive cultivation but, like their US counterparts, they do not themselves control *sales* on the international market. On the contrary, this is still dominated by US capital and US transnationals. Chase Manhattan Bank, through its Brazilian branches, has extended over US$100 million in loans for soya bean productions; and Cargill and Continental Grain, the world's two largest US grain traders, have set up multi-million dollar plants in Brazil that process soya beans for the export market.

Looking for Land

On the side of a road running through the southern state of Parana is a temporary encampment of Brazilian peasants who have lost their land either by force or by financial collapse. They are in search of alternative land, or perhaps some benefits from the recently announced land reform. But prospects are bleak.

continued

Antonio:

> I originally came from Minas Gerais, much further north from here. We grew beans, rice, and corn on 25 hectares of land. We had to leave because of mechanization that came and threw us off. I had to look for other resources, where there wasn't mechanization, for us to work with our hands. . .Mechanization isn't good for anyone, for the small people – it is only good for the big farmers. There have been no benefits so far from soya. If I want to eat vegetable oil, I have to pay the price they want – the grocery store owners. . . after soya started to be produced here there was less work. . . For the future I may buy a piece of land for the children to work so that they can have 'the bread of every day'.

His wife, Manuela:

> I hope to have a piece of land from the land reform and all my children close to me, a nice house and some animals, and a cow in order to have milk for the children. We need a school for the small children to study, and a church. I have faith and hope for the future.

Foreign capital quickly adapts to changing circumstances, breaking down national boundaries and helping to deepen the international division of labour. If Brazil produces soya beans cheaper than the USA, the giant trading firms move quickly into the Brazilian market to promote its exports around the world. They follow the old merchant's dictum of buying as cheap as possible and selling dear, no matter if their sales adversely affect soya producers in other parts of the world.

In the meantime, Brazilian landowners, though rich in relation to their workers, remain relatively weak in the world market. Brazil is the world's second largest agricultural exporter (after the USA), but its national capitalists play only a marginal role in world trade. Minute Maid, a Coca-Cola subsidiary, markets Brazilian orange juice abroad, Cargill exports soya beans, Anderson Clayton exports cotton, and General Foods buys a large share of Brazil's coffee beans. In the final analysis, Brazilian landowners seem to have only one means of strengthening their position in the world market – by intensifying their exploitation of the labour force.

Energy From the Land

In 1980, oil accounted for 40 per cent of Brazil's total energy consumption, even though almost all the electricity (9 per cent) was generated by hydroelectric power. Road and air transport remains essential to this vast country so, when the oil bill doubled in two years from 1978 to 1980, the government pressed ahead as fast as possible with the development of *ethanol* as a motor-vehicle fuel.

Ethanol is alcohol distilled from sugar cane. It now fuels about 90 per cent of the cars produced for the domestic market. Heavily subsidized by the government, it is cheaper at the pumps than petrol; but at current prices it costs more to produce 1 litre of ethanol than to import 1 litre of petrol. With the falling price of oil in the mid-1980s, some people have expressed serious reservations about the viability of ethanol.

But the programme has influential backers. Farmers who grow cane are increasingly dependent on government subsidies, while the world price of sugar is low; and the motor-car industry is subsidized to produce alcohol-compatible engines. In addition, fertilizer manufacturers sell to the plantation owners – and the middle classes want to run their cars cheaply.

As the demand for sugar increases, so too does the pressure on land. To maintain present targets, 5 million extra acres per year of sugar cane will have to be planted. In consequence, cane cutters who retain traditional plots of land will be under increasing pressure to give up that land and move to company houses.

The World Bank has contributed in the region of US$5 billion to Brazil's sugar programme. Privately, though, doubts have been aired. Since 1984, much smaller amounts have been allocated to credit schemes for small farmers in the North East, as the Bank begins to realize the devastating effects its investments have had on land rights. Violent disputes are common, resulting in many deaths from armed 'hit squads' employed by the owners. Few peasants are legally registered landowners, nor ever realized that they should be! As the harrassment of 'squatters' assumes ever greater importance in Brazil's turbulent political climate, the church in the North East has taken the lead in helping peasants claim their rights and resist eviction from landowners and speculators.

Cane cutters are entitled to up to 2 hectares of land by law, yet the courts have refused to return land to them once it has been taken away. Most peasants are illiterate and ignorant of their legal rights; their case has been taken up by rural workers' unions such as Fetape, but compensation cases apply only to destroyed crops, not to actual land lost. A programme of land reform is once, again, being touted as a solution, but it seems that the damage has already been done.

In essence, the sugar programme is built on cheap labour. Cane cutters are not paid a minimum wage; they are paid piecework rates. In the North East, this is currently about CRS18,000 (£1.15) per tonne cut and tied. On average, a man can expect to complete 1.5–2 tonnes a day, so his weekly wage is equivalent to £10; for women, it is less. But the harvest lasts only a short period, and this is often the *only* income s/he will receive all year.

In 1986, the Catholic Bishops of Brazil stated the case quite clearly:

> If we assume that the average family in the North-East consists of six people, there is no escaping the fact that the per capita income of at least 45% of North-Easterners was in 1983 2,550 cruzeiros a month, or 25 dollars a year, lower than any per capita income in any country on earth, and below the level of absolute poverty. There are constant reports of labourers dying of starvation and children of six months fed only on sugar and water.[15]

The people's response, at first faltering, is now growing in momentum. Street demonstrations, petitions and formal demands through trade unions, have made Brazilian rural workers ever more vocal in their quest for fundamental change. The principal demand is agrarian reform – an end to the deeply rooted structures of injustice and domination. The rural workers' union, Fetape, is attempting to turn spontaneous riots or isolated cases of violence into concerted political and legal action. But it is an uphill struggle. A union lawyer, Romen da Fonte, speaks of mill owners 'buying their way out of trouble' and conspiring with local government officials and police to remove any threat to their supremacy. Da Fonte's approach, whilst being thoroughly pragmatic, sadly reflects realities in Brazil today: 'In terms of justice, we have to avoid using the word. What we're actually talking about is legal procedures. Justice doesn't come into it.'

The Urban Crisis

The problems of providing food for the millions in the slums of Sao Paulo, Recife and Rio de Janeiro is beginning to worry the Brazilian government. Urban squalor means not only slums, poverty, unemployment and poor education; it also means the threat of unrest – an impending danger to the status quo. In the countryside, people are mostly disorganized and dispersed; in the towns, they are concentrated and potentially dangerous. The metropolitan population of Sao Paulo, for instance, is now around 13 million, growing at a rate of 175,000 a year. This is the 'city of promise', offering large rewards for initiative and enterprise; but as the tide turns, the *favelados* might soon realize that Brazil's miracle was never intended to touch them.

Precious resources have been shifted so that those crops grown for domestic consumption are transported to new centres of population. The urban middle classes in particular should be well-fed; for the poor, welfare hand-outs and promises attempt, unsuccessfully, to fill the gaps. In Rio de Janeiro, the city of the glamorous Copacabana beach and casinos, 1 million children survive by begging, stealing and child prostitution.

Tainted Cities

In search of the 'better life' of the city, José and his family moved to Sao Paulo in 1983

> because I had no land to work, and neither the employer nor the government appreciated our work. Conditions were bad because we had to pay the agricultural supplier 100 per cent more and sell 50 per cent cheaper. . . we were falling into an abyss carrying a heavy cross that we couldn't stand any more. . . When I arrived here it was quite fine, then after three to four years it got worse. The minimum wage I earned wasn't enough to support the children.   *continued*

> The conditions in the *favela* aren't good, because we live in a shack and there is a lot of garbage. It's not clean here – the municipality and the state don't offer us conditions to have a decent life. Here we are quite frightened, and there it was very peaceful. In the countryside farm we worked very much, but it was very peaceful. . .
>
> The future of Sao Paulo depends on the government and the support of the people. Sao Paulo can become the great and wonderful city that some people already talk about. It can welcome everybody, because everybody comes here and everybody is integrated. For me it is a wonderful city, but really I want to return to the land because here there is little work. People are very busy, very speedy. One works a lot, never saves money, and we keep on that way – we get the monthly wage, and we are broke again, keep on without anything. I tell other people not to come. Here it is only illusion. . . a big mess.

As the middle classes enjoyed Coca-Cola and ice cream, the price of rice and beans – the staple foods of the poor, rose by over 500 per cent from 1985–6. The official minimum wage of CRS600,000 (about £37) bears no relation to the true cost of living. Hunger is endemic in city slums: 25 million Brazilian children are undernourished. Fruit and vegetables are almost entirely absent from a poor family's diet and, in the *favelas*, high incidences of flu, fever, diarrhoea and worms are reported. Statistics reveal other levels of injustice: there is a marked tendency for girls to be worse-off than boys.[16]

Too many mouths to feed? The standard 'fix' was rolled out on disinfected trolleys – 2.3 million women sterilized in various parts of the country since 1973, courtesy of a US institution called Benfam, at the request of the Brazilian government. The Brazilian bishops have stated publicly that many women were unaware of the kind of operation they were undergoing.

After the 'Miracle': Brazil's future

On a warm April day in 1986, Father Josimo Moraes Tavares strolled towards the Church Commission's offices in the town of

Imperatriz, in the North East of Brazil. As he was mounting the steps, an unmarked car drew up alongside the commission and several shots were fired from the back seat. The wounded priest struggled to escape, but the attacker leapt from the car and finished his task with a single shot in Father Tavares's head.

Statistically, the killing was unremarkable: 261 deaths had been officially registered as 'land-battle' killings the previous year. The only unusual fact was that this was a priest, a man who had worked tirelessly on behalf of the poor and evicted peasants around Sao Sabastiao, his parish in the state of Marinhao. His death was widely reported. President Sarney himself expressed regret, launched an official inquiry and sent troops to the state 'to prevent violence'. Cynics may question his motives: on 9 July, the President flew to Rome to ask the Pope to mediate in the growing dispute with radical elements of the Catholic Church over land reform. The government were clearly unable to contain the spread of shootings since their tentative land redistribution programme launched in 1985. Even Sarney's own Cabinet were deeply split over the issue: the Minister for Agrarian Reform had resigned, complaining that the government showed no commitment to the programme.

Under the original land reform proposal, large estates were to be taken from their owners and divided among small farmers. The first year of the resettlement programme aimed at finding land for 150,000 families. Even the most optimistic projections see only 10 per cent of that figure being reached. Under pressure from landowners the reform plan was soon watered down by specifying that only non-productive landholdings would be commandeered, allowing property owners to make a rapid pretence of cultivating the land in order to escape the effects of the law.

More ominously, a militant landowners' organization, already some 5,000 strong, has been set up to resist these 'invasions' of property. In the state of Goias, 1,000 head of cattle were auctioned to raise money for guns. Farmers claim that murders by hired killers go unreported, and are often committed with the connivance of public authorities, including the police.

According to the government's own figures, Brazil's richest 10 per cent still hold 47 per cent of the national income and 7 per cent of the land. A recent report, *Brazil 2000* draws an alarming profile of chronic poverty and suggests that the country is reaching the limits of peaceful coexistence between rich and poor.[17] The issue of land reform is not simply an internal matter: it challenges the whole basis of an economic arrangement whereby wealth produced by the mass of people at the bottom is extracted, level by level, for the benefit of powerful business, both national and international.

As the gap between the 'two Brazils' widens, further violence seems almost inevitable as those who benefit from the status quo fight tooth and nail any attempt to upset the 'natural' balance. Less visibly, violence *already* exists – a daily violence against people in the form of malnutrition, joblessness and the diseases of poverty. As one observer noted, 'those who are responsible for murder by undernourishment are not locked inside, since they are the keepers of the keys.'[18]

6

Exporting Recession: The USA Pays the Price

> ashamed to be white,
> ashamed not to be in jail,
> why do I keep howling about:
>
> sky overcast with the colour of hunger,
> liars who kiss like arsenic sandpaper,
> white power gas, the torture game
> and the one-eyed glare of that final global flame?
>
> because they are here.
>
> Adrian Mitchell, *To the Silent Majority*

Norman Larson is 62 years old. He has been a farmer all his life, owning a piece of land just outside Worthington, Minnesota, in the heart of America's Mid-West. His great-grandfather bought it in 1871, and the family has worked there ever since – 'it's part of you, it's in the blood.' Two years ago, saddled with debt and a steady drop in the price of his crops, Norman was forced to let go; his farm was sold and he was bankrupt.

These buildings around here – I've helped build every one of 'em. . . those evergreens over there, I planted them probably 20 years ago; and that apple tree was planted when my father was still farming – I was probably 17–18 years old. . .it really hurts, hurts right in here, when you see the things you've worked so hard to get, then you come back and someone else is farming it. It's like they've taken part of your life. It's the way the economy has gone, not our fault.

For the Larson family, and many thousands like them, the issue runs deeper than just a loss of land. A whole way of life for

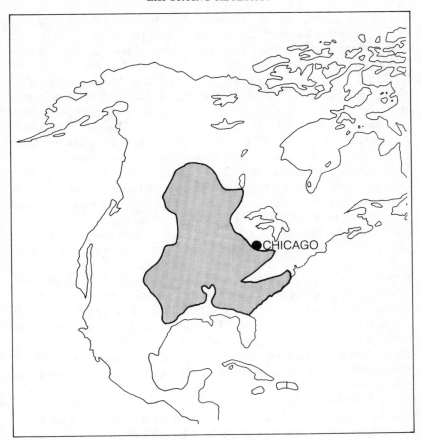

Figure 10 The farming region of North America

traditional farming communities is rapidly giving way to massive industrial agriculture. The result is structural crisis, a change in attitudes, and a breakdown in social convention. David Benson, one of the few remaining small farmers, explains:

> The way things are now, there's no room for mistakes. I mean, one false judgment is enough to jeopardize your whole farming career. I feel society is becoming more inhospitable to any differences. If you're not right on track with this industrialized agriculture, you're just not gonna exist. It's a frightening thing for me to see, it really is.

What is the nature of 'industrialized' agriculture and why is it fundamentally changing the nature of food production? So far, we have concentrated on hunger in the South and the manner in which 'imported' food systems are grafted on to traditional societies by foreign or indigenous elites. We have seen how these systems fail so spectacularly in the one simple job that is required of them – that they feed all people within a given society. A ubiquitous demonstration of what Susan George calls 'inauthentic' models of production is the fact that so many countries in the world are unable to solve their food problem and depend on increased imports.[1]

But Norman Larson and David Benson live in the grain-rich prairies of America's Mid-West. If the tell-tale signs of crisis are becoming evident even here, then surely the whole system of food production in the North, as well as the South, is brought into question? Bankruptcy is only one part of a whole spectrum of disorder: a high incidence of poverty and hunger in the world's richest countries are further reasons to fundamentally question what is going on. Why is it that in Europe and the USA increasing numbers of people go without a sufficient daily intake of calories? The figures are staggering: in the USA alone, some 20 million people do not have enough to eat.[2] Harsh reality is invariably buried beneath the rhetoric of 'progress' and 'growth', a blind faith that capitalism will provide for each according to his needs. Yet, even in the rich North, wide cracks are beginning to appear in the social fabric.

Food Systems: North and South

Our image of farming in rich industrial countries is usually determined by where we live and how old we are. The move from small-scale peasant production to large farms, hired labour and modern equipment has come about gradually over a long period of time. Combine harvesters, large machinery and single-crop cultivation may be more familiar to the younger generation; but, as recently as the 1950s, horse-drawn ploughs were used on some farms in Britain, and still are in certain East European countries. There is, however, one striking feature of post-war agriculture, both in the North *and* the developing South that is a distinctly 'modern' invention: that is, the increased *productivity* – output per person – that comes from treating food as a saleable commodity for a world market, rather than a domestic 'eat as you grow' product.

A food system is the total means whereby a human community goes about feeding itself. Food systems can be varied, but each have three basic sectors:

1   *Inputs* – such as seed, machinery, fertilizers, etc..

2   *Agricultural Production* – the actual work that goes into farming.

3   *Post-Harvest Activities* – including storage, distribution and marketing; everything that happens between the field and the supermarket shelf.

Although there is no distinctive Southern food system, most developing countries rely on their one most abundant resource: human labour. Land may be poor, but labour is rich: between 50 and 90 per cent of the populations of the South are involved in agriculture – the direct opposite of the richer North.

Broadly speaking, traditional food systems in the South managed in the past to meet peoples' needs while remaining environmentally sound. Until recently, sectors 1 and 3 – inputs and post-harvest activities – were not capital intensive. Animal power, simple tools and reproduced seeds were all that were required; and the producers and consumers were often one and the same. Colonialism, as we have seen, changed this system dramatically by introducing wage (or slave) labour on plantations growing for an export market. The dependence on foreign exchange continued to determine food policies after independence, putting further pressure on traditional systems.

Most Southern nations are today locked in a state of dependency on high-production methods of agriculture for cash. Agribusiness corporations are invited to advise governments on the best way to increase yields and sell their goods on the world market. These corporations are aided and abetted by international aid, which lays down the necessary infrastructure – roads, electric power, etc. Higher productivity invariably means either less labour (causing massive migration to the cities), or unacceptably cheap labour (causing undernourishment and susceptibility to famines). The imposition of Northern-style food systems in the South actually

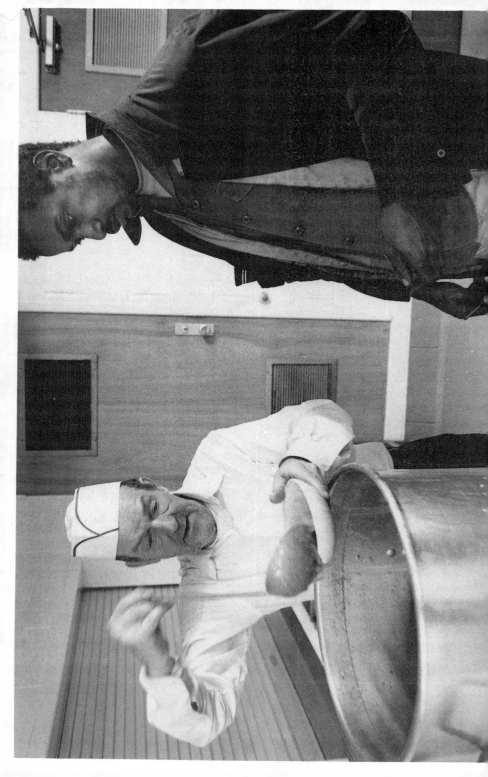

increases disparities in wealth between North and South, and between rich and poor in the receiving country.

In the industrial countries themselves, great changes have also occurred during the course of the twentieth century. More weight is given to sectors 1 and 3 of the food system than ever before. Fewer and fewer people actually work the land – in Britain and the USA only 1–2 per cent of the population produce the food that feeds the rest. Size of landholdings and net output is also highly concentrated: in the USA, for example, one-third of the farms produce 90 per cent of the food.

The Family Farmer

I think there is a growing idea that family farmers are like white baby seals. We need to put them in a museum and think about them fondly, but they are of the past. That is a romantic view that does not reflect reality – that family farmers are highly efficient producers, that they are the backbone of a rural community's economic viability. . .
The University of California spent millions of dollars developing this Northern California Olive-Growing mechanized programme and the pesticides. They spent zero dollars looking at the impact of that programme on family farms, on labour, on consumers, on environmental questions.

Elizabeth Martin, California Institute of Rural Studies, 1986

This concentration in production – the high-technology model of agriculture – may, on the face of it, seem highly effective. After all, if 2.5 million American farmers can produce enough to feed 250 million people, leaving millions of tons for exports besides, then surely as a model of efficiency it has no equal? Such figures, though, disguise real costs – in subsidies, imported foodstuffs and tax incentives, not to mention environmental decay. In addition, the USA faces a national crisis measured more easily in human than

---

Soup kitchen in the land of plenty – an embarrassing post-script to the American Dream
Roger Hutchings/Network

economic terms: more than one-third of all farmers in the bread-basket states of the Mid-West are heading for bankruptcy. Lyle Adolph, a farmer in Minnesota, puts the matter in perspective: 'Seems like most of the farm places now have non-farmers living in them; the people are working in the cities. This morning I was looking at a map of our township, which is 6 miles wide and 6 miles long. Today we have 40 farmers on those 36 square miles; years ago we had 135 farmers on that same land.'

The quest for greater productivity lies at the heart of an 'expand or die' approach to farming. There is a rigid belief that the 'market' will be self-regulating, and that competition for that market can only come about through a spread of competing private businesses. The overriding concern is for profit and steady expansion to 'keep up' with leaders in the field. The USA consumes only two-thirds of what it produces; so farmers are also under pressure to export, thus facing further competition from other countries.

All this costs a great deal in capital investment – in seeds, fertilizers, research and labour-saving machinery. Despite rising food prices, it has become increasingly difficult for small and medium-size farms to break even; they are being squeezed constantly between rising costs of production and falling prices for farm products. Farmers in the USA who, before the war, spent about half their income on capital investments, now spend over 80 per cent. In Britain, about 75 million a year is spent to increase production in this way.

To minimize costs, farmers must increase landholdings, usually at the expense of their smaller neighbours. Many struggle desperately to keep their heads above water, and sink deeper into debt. In the USA, this particularly affects the 700,000 or so full-time farmers who grow between US$50,000 and US$200,000 worth of produce a year on farms of 400–800 acres. Banks are less willing to extend credit, and often the only option is to sell up.

So sector 2 of the food system – that which involves human labour – is, in the USA, beginning to mirror the kind of changes so widespread in the developing world: unemployment, displacement and out-migration to cities. The social casualties of debt and foreclosure are evident across the mid-West farm belt. In Missouri, suicide amongst farmers is higher than in any other occupation; crisis hotlines have opened, offering financial and emotional counselling; and, outside the courthouses, symbolic white wooden crosses are planted to mark by, way of protest, properties that have been auctioned off. The era of the small farmer is drawing to a close.

Too Much of a Good Thing

It might be argued that increasing concentration of land lends itself to greater efficiency in output, and that the passing of the small farmer is a regrettable, but inevitable, price of progress. Perhaps so, but this begs the question of who benefits from higher yields. When we look at agricultural policies in the industrial North, we are faced with glaring paradoxes. In the USA, the government pays farmers not to grow grain; it subsidizes irrigation and land clearance projects, then pays the owners not to use the land for growing crops. Across the Atlantic in Europe, farmers are paid artificially inflated prices to produce surpluses that nobody wants; and the EEC pays producers 18 cents for a pound of sugar, sells it on the world market for 5 cents, then *imports* someone else's sugar – at 18 cents a pound![3]

The 12-nation EEC spends US$63,000 an hour to store 1.4 million tons of unsold butter in refrigerated warehouses. Its mountain of skimmed milk weighs almost 1 million tons. Agricultural output has been growing four times as fast as food consumption – the beautiful curse of high-technology production.

Only 10 years ago, surpluses of this kind were seen as a temporary blessing for farmers as they bolstered their income by providing for an expanding world-wide market. Banks were lending generously to the developing world, who then went on a food-buying spree. Farmers everywhere cashed in on the new prosperity. Very soon, however, the tables turned. Debt in the South, the 'Green Revolution', and world-wide recession led to shrinking overseas markets. Today, Europe's surpluses have become a huge albatross around the neck of EEC ministers.

So why don't they simply give away the food surpluses? The tragedy of starvation in the midst of plenty points not only to incompetency, but also moral bankruptcy on the part of so many world leaders. In 1986, the USA had carryover stocks of 85 million tons of grain; the EEC had 20 million tons, Canada 13 million, and Australia 7 million.[4] According to the FAO, EEC surpluses alone could have provided the food needs of 21 of the worst-affected drought countries in Africa in 1985. There is, then, no problem of

food stocks, but they are not where they ought to be. Why? Because the financial interests of the North continue to outweigh the urgency to set up an effective safety net for the South.

This is not to say that giving away grain surpluses would solve the problem; the issue is far more complex than a simple matter of distribution. A flood of free grain would destroy countless producers in the South, as has happened in certain 'famine priority' countries. For the EEC and the USA, it is a question of finance: those countries that most need the food can least afford to pay for it. In 1986, the price of a bushel of grain had fallen to only US$3.25, compared with US$4.43 in 1978. As Brussels and Washington, who between them control 60 per cent of the world market, struggle to undercut each other, the price could fall even further. This may be encouraging to some importers in the South but, for most, the price is still prohibitive. Food aid, when it is used, usually goes to 'friendly' governments who can then sell it to help offset their balance of payment difficulties. But there is plenty of evidence that food aid increases dependency and binds developing countries more tightly to the dominant economic system of the North.

Agro Action

You now have some people who are coming through all this, who are going to Washington and saying: we can't stand this anymore. You've got bankers and others standing alongside them – a very exciting development where farmers and rural people considered the most conservative, the 'rednecks' of the past, are now up front saying: what is wrong with the system when people who give their lives, and work this hard, are thrown off with nothing? They're challenging notions of free enterprise; they're talking about how we affect the Third World. They are, in fact, leading a whole new upsurge of political movement in this country, unlike anything we've seen since the 60s.

Mark Ritchie, Special Advisor, Minnesota Department of Agriculture
continued

High-technology agriculture in the USA: a blessing or a curse?
Carlos Reyes/Andes Press Agency

> I'm concerned about my grandchildren, and everybody
> else's grandchildren, and I don't ever want them to say:
> 'Hey, Grandpa, you had a chance to turn it around – why
> didn't you?' And that's why I'm in here fighting.
>
> Norman Larson, US farmer, 1986

In contrast to, say, the Horn of Africa, bankrupt farmers in the USA do not starve to death. But their ill-fortune is inextricably linked to that of their counterparts on the hillsides of Ethiopia. If we wish critically to examine the dominant food system that oils the wheels of the hunger machine, we must first take a long hard look at the interests that lie behind it. In whose interest is it to produce *too much* food in the North, whilst ensuring that farmers in the South do not even grow sufficient for their daily needs? And why, in spite of those surpluses, are we unable (or unwilling) to provide the means to fully support our own people, let alone those of the South? Food stamps in the USA, supplementary benefit in Britain, and widespread urban malnutrition in both, are sober reminders that our own house is not in order.

Transatlantic Grain War

Huge food surpluses on both sides of the Atlantic have intensified the underhand war of hidden protectionism. The USA has begun to look increasingly to the world market to get rid of its over-produced grain. By subsidizing export prices – that is, by keeping the price of grain low on the world market through federal support for farmers in the grainbelt – it has entered the fray with a vengeance, and is heading for a bitter trade war with Europe, and also less fortunate 'friends' such as Thailand.

The EEC attained a comfortable position in world agricultural sales in the 1970s. Today, however, it faces an intractable mess. World recession and the enormous debts of the South have shrunk traditional markets for crop surpluses. Like their American counterparts, Europe's farmers have become victims of their own success. The EEC is now self-sufficient in most major agricultural categories, but its produce is expensive and can only be disposed of with the help of huge subsidies. The use of such subsidies has set it on a collision course with the USA, Canada, Australia, and Argentina.

What Price Trade Principles?

I believe that the US. . . is not primarily taking markets away from other exporters. The main attempt is actually being made to take away markets from local producers, often in poor countries. What the US is basically doing is trying to offer what we call fire sale prices – extremely low prices for our exports – in hopes of taking markets around the world. . . Europe, Saudi Arabia and Japan protect farmers at their borders; but the the impact really comes in the Third World. We're able to go into a country and sell our produce below the cost of production for the local farmer.

Mark Ritchie, Minnesota Department of Agriculture

If you are an exporter, and your policy gets somewhat out of balance with supply and demand, then I think you need to stop and take a look at that policy and say: Aren't we really purchasing our own security at the expense of others?

Robbin Johnson, Vice President, Cargill

The political stakes are very high on both sides of the Atlantic. In Europe, the Common Agricultural Policy (CAP), for all its excesses, is upheld by left- and right-wing governments. It has relieved EEC countries of their dependency on food imports and slowed the depopulation of the countryside. Four times as many Europeans as Americans still call themselves farmers – a powerful constituency. Similarly, farm policy in the USA is political dynamite: Washington has been pushed to take protectionist measures and to subsidize exports so that they can compete in markets the Europeans have 'unfairly' captured.

Liberalizing Agriculture: Is it Possible?

The obvious long-term solution to absurd overproduction in Northern countries would be to knock out price supports and force farmers to grow no more than customers at home and overseas have the money and desire to buy. International economic conferences are currently exploring new initiatives of this kind. Famine, debt, and continuing imbalance in favour of industrial countries, have given added impetus to the call for a 'liberalization' of agriculture; that is, the opening up of a 'free market' in world agriculture.

Industrialized Countries

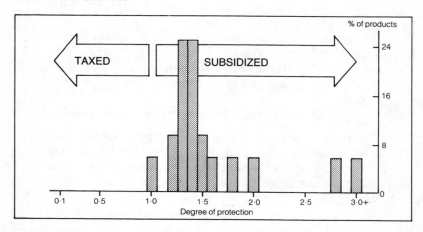

Developing Countries

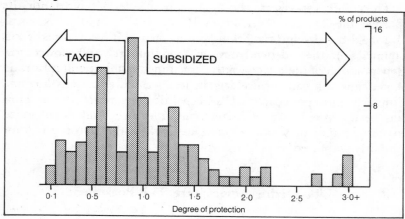

Figure 11 World food output subsidization and taxation
Source: World Bank, 1984

On the face of it, both developing and industrial countries would benefit from liberalized agricultural trade. The World Bank estimates that if all countries exposed their farmers to world market prices for major food items – grain, rice, meat and dairy products – the combined national incomes of the South would rise by US$18 billion annually, while Northern countries would gain US$46 billion.[5] The only losers, by a margin of US$23 billion a year, would be the Eastern bloc countries (excluding China): they are the biggest beneficiaries of US and European dumping of food surpluses on the world market.

Such calculations seem to present a straightforward case for liberalizing international trade. Or so it seems, until one begins to look closer at the political implications. What would be the immediate result of the USA lifting farm subsidies? Or of the lifting of farm tax in, say, Nigeria?

In the USA, farm exports have dropped from US$43.8 billion in 1981 to US$26.5 billion in 1986. This is not only due to a shrinking world market, but also to a vast welfare system for the agricultural industry which, in spite of President Reagan's instinctive preference for a return to free market principles, has kept US prices relatively high, so buyers are more difficult to find. The same thing has happened in Japan: farmers each year grow more rice than the nation's citizens can eat; yet rice can be sold only under government licence, and consumers pay about three times the average world price to buy it.

The drive to produce greater and more profitable (subsidized) amounts of food is only achievable through massive investment and capital – that is, it is beyond the reach of small farmers in Europe, the USA, or Japan. So it is not the poorer family farmer who gains from agricultural protection and subsidy; rather, it is the large industrial farms that benefit disproportionately from high prices. Even more important, it is the *owners*, not the tillers who gain from these policies. Their political voice is much stronger than that of poorer consumers who push their trolleys around the supermarkets of Europe and the USA.

If state subsidies were dropped, consumer prices of basic foodstuffs in Northern countries would also drop initially. Because farm prices as they stand today would be too low, many farmers would be ruined. It is likely that, after a period of time, prices would again rise, and the USA (and a few other suppliers) would again dominate the market. We can only speculate as to the final outcome; what is certain is that farmers, though few in number, retain enough political clout to prevent any such drastic measures. In the USA, they and those dependent on them (small-town bankers, food processors, machinery makers, and the like) dominate the economies of enough states to wield disproportionate power in Congress. One result of this was that, in 1986, the Reagan administration drew US$26 million from tax-payers' money to keep farmers in business.

In the South, almost the exact opposite is the case. Governments currently pay their farmers *below* world market prices for their goods, thus effectively subsidizing food prices for the relatively better-off urban consumers. More importantly, agriculture is taxed and is frequently a major source of state income. Liberalizing agriculture would involve three important changes: first, prices paid to farmers would rise, and food in urban centres like Rio de Janeiro, Khartoum or Manila would cost more; second, any remaining subsidies would have to be targeted to the poorest urban consumers; third, alternative sources of tax revenue would have to be found, most probably tax on land values – a policy directed more towards rich landowners than poor peasants.

For many regimes in the South, though, it is not only a question of taking wealth from one sector of the population and giving it to another. Modern industrial agriculture, cash-cropping and new manufacturing industries, have swelled the number of people moving into large cities, from Rio de Janeiro to Lagos, to Calcutta. If paying higher prices to farmers also means putting up the price of grain in the towns, this may trigger unrest, particularly amongst poorer slum dwellers who have little to lose. Pragmatic political calculations have to be made: urban tension is a great deal less desirable than rural poverty, for it threatens the political power base of Southern elites.

So, the options for a restructuring of world agriculture look distinctly unattractive to those in whose hands agricultural policy lies. Political reality is such that domestic considerations in all countries, North and South, will continue to outweigh any commitment to a more efficient use of the world's resources. The issue at stake is individual and corporate wealth – and, in some cases, national security – not free market policy as such. This does, at least, explain why the distortions of international agricultural policy have proved so enduring.

For our purposes here, we have followed through the possible outcome of a 'free market' in world agriculture, simply as a theoretical model. But the sad fact is that farmers, governments, tax-payers and the poor will probably continue to pay the price of high subsidies and ruthless competition – and waste million of tons of food. This year, the EEC produced a surplus of wine big enough to fill 1,500 Olympic swimming pools. There is, indeed, a 'crisis' in world capitalism when the simple logic of supply and demand – the economics of the market place – gives way to such excesses.

The Grain Trade

Not far from the struggling farming community of Worthington, Minnesota, is a large luxurious French-style chateau, headquarters of Cargill Inc., the biggest privately owned US corporation. This is the nerve-centre of one of the world's most widely spread empires. Cargill is a name not well known to the public, but it is well known to the farmer. It's business is the buying, shipping and selling of grain, millions of tons of it every year.

Cargill is the largest single contributor to the US balance of payments, yet it is run by just two families, who hold 85 per cent of the stock. The company is one of the 'big five' who between them have an almost total monopoly of the US grain trade and, hence, a huge share in the world market. The other four companies are Continental Grain (USA), Bunge (Argentina), Dreyfus (France) and André-Garnac (Switzerland). All are private, and are controlled by single families who do not have to answer to shareholders.

The phenomenal expansion of US agriculture in the 1970s enabled the 'big five' to extend their operations far beyond the grain trade – into meat packing, poultry, seed production, soya beans and sugar trading. Cargill now operates in 36 different countries through its subsidiary, Tradax, based in Geneva. Tradax mirrors Cargill in all its overseas activities. It now has offices in Manila, Tokyo, Panama, Buenos Aires, Amsterdam and London.

From 1970 to 1980, the world grain trade increased 2.5 times, from about 80 million tons to 200 million tons a year. The USA captured three-quarters of the new market. Those who really

The American Bread-Basket

I think many American farmers believe they are feeding the world, no matter how much they are sacrificing. Fundamentally, there are several misunderstandings in this notion. First of all, the bulk of our agricultural exports – certainly the majority of our edible exports – don't go to feeding human beings, they go to feed livestock. We could say that the US is not the bread-basket, but the restauranteur of the world, meaning that our exports go to feed a class of people who can afford to eat grain-fed meat. You find in the world today that the market place demand for feed grains is going up about 75 per cent higher than the demand for food, because hungry people are unable to demand what they need. So that should begin to tell us something.

Another misunderstanding is that the US bread-basket image suggests that people in the Third World simply don't have the resources to feed themselves. The truth is, those resources are available, but people just don't have access to them. In many countries, such as India with a surplus of 24 million tons, the food already exists. So we must go beyond this notion of the US feeding the world.

Frances Moore Lappé, Co-Founder of the US Institute
for Food and Development Policy

benefited were companies whose profit depends on the number of bushels transported and sold to overseas bidders. A company like Cargill, for instance, does not own land; therefore it is not susceptible to falling grain prices, poor weather or land mortgages. It is an intermediary in the commodity market and usually profits regardless of calamities the farmers may be facing. Through astute investment, particularly in transport and storage in the late 1960s, Cargill was able to anticipate the forthcoming boom and, in a word, make a mint.

Crucially, Cargill controls the means of transport for much of America's grain. The sheer scale of its operation – a fleet of 500 barges, 5,000 rail cars and 14 ocean-going vessels – enables the corporation to offer better prices to farmers and to its overseas customers, thus undercutting many cooperatively owned local businesses. Furthermore, through access to the Chicago commodity markets, it can predict fairly accurately any changes in market forces and adjust accordingly. Large profits can be made on the futures market before farmers themselves know what has happened.

Frances Moore Lappé, co-founder of the Institute for Food and Development Policy, recognizes the dilemma facing the small farmer in the USA:

> When farmers go to buy what they need, whether it be machines or fertilizers, they're confronted with a handful of suppliers. They have no bargaining power when it comes to their necessary supplies. Likewise, when they go to sell their commodities, they have no bargaining power, because there are a handful of trading corporations that deal in the world marketing of their grain. So farmers are squeezed between two very monopoly-controlled sectors. Here you see parallels with the Third World: the only people who are surviving are those who have enough wealth and land, and can keep growing to make up in volume what they're losing in profits per acre.

False Promises?

The rush for the export market in the 1970s and the resulting concentration of land led to the 'mining' of valuable resources and a narrow specialization in single crops that is now beginning to be questioned, particularly by the ecology lobby. Farmers are increasingly vulnerable to international price fluctuations and, by the early 1980s, they were facing the worst financial collapse since the Great Depression.

US Department of Agriculture policy is to keep grain prices low to try to make US exports more competitive. At the same time, it hopes to boost volume. This is, however, a finite game: overall demand for world grain very soon levels out. The USA already ships 80 per cent of the world's soya beans, 70 per cent of the corn, and 40 per cent of the wheat. The recent drop in demand is inevitably affecting the

growth rate of large corporations, as well as the livelihood of
farmers. How are they protected? Robbin Johnson, Vice-President
of Cargill Inc:

> We take the long view. We have the advantage of not only
> private ownership but a commitment to look past the cyclical
> swings and make our decisions on investments and what future
> business we'll be in based on longer time-horizons.
>
> I think the grain trade is a good business. If you look at basic
> forces that drive this business, there are three: growth in world
> population, growth in per capita incomes, and growth in
> specialization in the world economy. . . as those three things go
> on, there'll continue to be growing opportunities for grain to
> move from surplus-producing countries to deficit countries.
> And that's our business.

Such optimism is echoed by the US Department of Agriculture.
Washington USDA Under-Secretary, Goldberg, puts on a brave
face:

> Crisis? It depends on where you are and who you're talking to.
> You get pockets of the country where there's real problems.
> You know, we're not sitting here in Washington unaware that
> there are a lot of farmers in deep financial trouble. . .There
> isn't anything we do in this country that's more productive and
> efficient than American agriculture, and although perceptually
> we're sagging a little right now, I think better times are
> coming.

In the meantime, the US administration is walking a tightrope,
attempting to trim and patch an over-inflated subsidy system whilst
erecting a hugely expensive greenhouse around farming, to insulate
it from the real world. The ploy is, to a large extent, political; but
how long will it last? Mark Ritchie, of the Minnesota Department of
Agriculture, is aware of the contradictions:

> The United States now spends about US$6 billion a year on
> deficiency payment subsidies to our corn producers. That
> subsidy is primarily, in the rhetoric of the administration, to
> help make us competitive in corn exports. Yet those corn
> exports are worth, in total, only US$3.5 billion! There is no
> economic sense in this; it is purely ideological.

Ideological or not, nations of the South have already developed a keen taste for American grain. Since the Second World War, US corporations have used Public Law 480 to open up new markets. Regular food-aid shipments, other than emergency supplies, come under the PL 480 agreement whereby recipient governments are allowed to sell the grain to generate income at home. Crucially, this whets local appetites for white flour, displaces home products, and often costs more to the consumer for lower nutritional value. In Sudan, for instance, it is considered a sign of prosperity and good manners to serve white bread to guests, rather than the more nutritious *dura* bread. More than 300,000 tons of PL 480 wheat flour pours into the country each year.

Picking Cotton

Export growth has not only affected American farmers, it has also hit farm labourers, particularly those in the Southern states. Stella Stamps and her husband have lived in the state of Mississippi all their lives. Cotton picking is still the main source of employment, a tough job in the blazing heat of the delta of America's Deep South. If they find work, they consider themselves lucky.

We can earn maybe US$35 a day, when we can get it. There are a lot fewer jobs than there used to be, because of mechanization – there ain't much work left these days. We have no running water in the house, but we don't want to move to the town or head north, like so many others. My husband's out looking for work just now. Sometimes he gets a truck to repair or something like that. More often, he gets nothing.

Ecological Hazards

Exploitation of land in the USA for short-term profit has meant that farms have been losing two bushels of topsoil for every bushel of corn produced. By 1985, it was estimated that the country had irrevocably lost a third of its valuable topsoil, primarily through the cutting of hedgerows and natural woodland borders.

Soil erosion is not the only threat to the environment. Continual planting reduces the land's fertility, leading to a greater dependency on chemical fertilizers, with rapidly diminishing returns. Crop monoculture – acres and acres of the same produce – also plays havoc with the natural ecosystem: bird, fungi and insect species disappear whilst others multiply – and increase the need for expensive pesticides.

Whilst creating conditions for costly financial credit, agrochemicals have caused an actual *fall* in output since the mid-1970s. Even more ominous is the narrowing of the genetic base of US crops. Six kinds of maize (corn) make up 70 per cent of US production, and just two kinds of peas account for 96 per cent of the US harvest. Because scientifically developed seeds often stem from only one or two genetic sources, the new varieties have less resistance to disease. Again, there is greater dependence on seed companies: genetically uniform harvests cannot be replanted the next year.

Not surprisingly, some farmers are beginning to wonder where American agriculture is heading. The Benson family run a small 160 acre farm near Worthington, Minnesota, on which they actively attempt to diversify crops, in stark contrast to most of their neighbours. David Benson surveys the land around him with unease:

> What you see behind me is the last remnant of the virgin prairie that comprised the whole of this country – just 14 acres, the last unbroken section. There are probably upward of 200 species on these 14 acres. Farmers around here have managed to replace it with a culture that only emphasizes 2 or 3 species. The land itself has been here since the glaciers; the white man has only been here 100 years, and we've eroded about half the topsoil. Let's hope we can do better in the next 100 years!

Extracting water from underground reservoirs is a less apparent, but no less alarming, aspect of modern agriculture. Canals dug in California, for instance, threaten not only wildlife variety, but also the actual quantity of water available for human consumption. Interesting similarities can be drawn with Sudan's Jonglei Canal project, an attempt by the Sudanese government to increase its Nile water allocation with unknown long-term risks to the Sahelian environment (see chapter 3).

Finally, the production of high-yield grain in the USA absorbs huge amounts of energy, mostly in the form of petroleum. The energy required to feed one person in the USA is more than 310 gallons of petroleum a year. If we were to attempt to feed the entire world's population at that level of energy consumption, all known petroleum supplies would be used up in about 10 years. For small farmers in the USA, the cost is too much to bear; one of the more poignant reminders of financial collapse in the grainbelt is scrapyards replete with unwanted combine harvesters.

Human Costs of High Technology

To recap, a food system comprises three main elements – inputs, actual production, and post-harvest activities. In the USA, as in Europe, the true test of the high-technology model is its ability to provide a suitable diet for all its citizens. Apart from the well-documented negative health aspects of the so-called 'affluent diet', there is ample evidence to suggest that the food system we have created in the North fails its last crucial test: malnutrition and outright starvation are now increasingly prevalent in the North.

A Long Way from the Potato

Americans are perhaps the only people on earth privileged to buy unbreakable perfectly calibrated, dehydrated, rehydrated parabolic potato chips packed in vacuum-sealed tennis ball cans – at dozens of times the cost of the original, long-forgotten potato.

Susan George, *Feeding the Few*

Food assistance programmes in the USA cost the tax-payer close to US$10 billion annually. Somewhat ironically, government-supported Food Stamps are used to buy supermarket products, thus increasing profits for the American food industry. The 50 or so companies dominating the food-processing industry not only benefit from selling their highly elaborate products on the supermarket

shelves, but also give away unwanted food to welfare organizations. The first food-assistance programmes were established not because people were hungry, but because there were surplus commodities to get rid of.

Even so, hunger and malnutrition, especially in rural areas, has increased in the last decade. Chicago, the USA's third largest city with a population of 3.5 million, houses thousands of migrants on its westside. Many are black people from the Southern states who came in search of the affluence of the North. The American Dream is here replaced by queues for the 'food box' outside local churches. In addition, the state-supported food stamp system supplements welfare cheques. When the bills are paid, the only flexibility in a family's budget is the quantity and quality of food purchased. Linette Cole and her son face the same problem every month:

> In the middle of the month, when our food stamps are gone, that's when I'm trying to get some cheese. You can maybe go to the store down the street and get a small loaf of bread for 39 cents. And you can make cheese sandwiches with some powdered milk, if you can afford some. It's better than nothing.

According to medical and nutritional experts, the US health budget could be cut by up to one-third (US$70 billion) if North Americans improved their diet. Dietary habits are, of course, conditioned by advertising and what people are able to buy. In areas such as Chicago's westside, it is a question of basic economics. Even if they are receiving public assistance, unemployment and the uncertainty of food prices means that some people cannot purchase food on a continuing and consistent basis.

In Their Own Words

> I'm not sure I'll make it, if it stays like this. When I'm at home I got all these roaches around here, I got 'em in my bed. You got rats; you can clean up all day long, but they're still there. The landlords know you don't have no
> *continued*

The Benson family on their farm in Minnesota: trying to break even in an era when small farmers are being squeezed out.
Mark Galloway

money to move, so they can do whatever they want. So they kept my kitchen ceiling like this, water pouring down on me all night long. I just have to mop and mop, so the house don't drown out. And then people want to know why I'm depressed.

Linette Cole, Chicago, 1986

All the time I worry about the Department of Human Services come knocking on my door, telling me I'm not feeding my kids the right food, or about me not having a stove. It really shakes me up sometimes, you know, I get to crying and stuff, because I don't have the things to give my kids. So I have to go to organizations to get funds. When I'm walking down the street to get my food box, I feel happy about, because it's better than nothing, see. Some people might not accept it, but I turn down nothing. [Laughs] I turn down no food.

Yollanda de Preto, Chicago, 1986

Dr Agnes Lattimer is medical director of Cook County Hospital in Chicago, which has seen an increased admission of young malnourished children in recent years:

Failure to thrive is malnutrition when it is associated with inadequate food intake. This means that a child is not growing at the proper rate; it can be associated with an increased susceptibility to infection and, in older children, an impairment of their ability to learn. We may not see youngsters actually starving today, but they're dying early as a secondary result of malnutrition.

We should be wary of statistics. Malnourishment in the USA is, of course, by no means on the same *scale* as in many countries of the South. The average cost of food per person, rated against income, is the lowest in the world. What gets lost in those averages, however, is the fact that the bottom 20 per cent or so spend as much on food in proportion to their income as many people in poorer countries. Income disparity in the USA is perhaps even more stark than elsewhere: in a society of fast food and hypermarkets, thousands simply do not have the income to afford the abundance potentially available to them.

The psychological aspects of the problem are perhaps even more revealing in a country that prides itself on being the most 'advanced' in the world. The prevailing philosophy is that if you are poor, there is something wrong with you, you are deficient in some way. Doctors complain that public support programmes tend to demean the participants to the point where they have to be desperate to avail themselves of the assistance they are entitled to. It is a question of self-respect and dignity, something echoed in Britain where each year millions of pounds worth of welfare is not taken up either through ignorance or this sort of social taboo.

Dr Shirley works at the Jackson Health Centre, Mississipi. He and other leading American doctors have prepared the most comprehensive recent national survey on hunger. The findings of the Physicians Task Force were startling:

> There are probably more, but we have been able to document at least 20 million individuals in this country that are hungry, that go without sufficient daily intake of calories or vitamins. . . It's tragic and unbelievable that we grow enough food in this country to feed every individual over and over. As a physician, I'm exposed to the consequences of a lack of care on the part of national government. We have the resources, we have everything but the will and desire to do something about it. We read a lot about national defence in terms of missiles, bombs and bullets; but I think chronic malnutrition is more of a threat to this nation than the Russians or Nicaraguans. We will end up with a generation – or maybe two or three generations, depending on how long this lasts – of individuals who have not grown intellectually or physically to their full potential. It will weaken this country.

The Transfer of Folly

We have, then, a food system in the North whose prestige and productive capacity is beginning to be overshadowed by economic, ecological and humanitarian pitfalls. The system itself is scientifically crude – the industrial production of greater yields for maximum market prices. And only the fittest survive: the big farmers, agrochemical industries and the grain trade barons.

Parallels with the poorer South are increasingly apparent: fewer and fewer people control greater amounts of land; absentee landowners – a landed 'aristocracy' – is beginning to emerge; and the cost is measured in terms of joblessness as rural communities are gutted. Here, as in the developing world, wages are inappropriate to the needs of struggling families, and a reckless disregard for conservation bodes ill for future generations.

But let us return for a moment to basics. What is 'technology', this so-called 'product' that not only dominates Northern food systems, but also is 'transferred' to ever-receptive developing nations? The first important point is that modern technology is not so much a product as a *process* and, as such, it cannot be 'neutral'. It is the result of centuries of developing capitalism, the embodiment of a specific social and economic process. Throughout this long period, scientific innovation stood back to back with political struggle. Technology incorporated relationships between social classes; it was geared to the needs of a social system in which one (smaller) group dominated another (much larger) group.

The basic outline of this Northern system has become increasingly refined, so much so that the 'social' elements of technology are now almost invisible. But they are still there, and still eminently exportable. The most fundamental tenet of modern industrial technology is, and has always been, the subjugation of human needs to that of private profit. Why else would so many industrial clashes from the Chartists to the 1984/5 British Miners' strike centre on the defence of people's jobs against their replacement by 'rationalized' (i.e. cheaper) mechanization or closure? And would US farmworkers have 'chosen' the replacement of human labour by machines, so that hundreds lose their jobs or face bankruptcy every year?

The technology developed in the North represents a whole series of choices, for the most part dictated by a powerful minority whose goal is to accrue power and profit, usually at the expense of the majority. This is not crude politicking; for what might have been the alternatives, given our levels of expertise? Instead of 34 million unemployed in the OECD countries (Europe and North America), we could have developed labour-intensive technologies. Instead of chemical food additives for long shelf-life and greater profits, or processed junk foods, we could have provided an abundant, healthy diet for all. Instead of the Bhopal Disaster, or Three Mile Island, we could have had technologies safe to work with.

Keeping a Tab on the Labels

The Group of 77 poorest nations of the South pointed out at the UN Conference on Science and Technology, that 90 per cent of the patents granted, supposedly, to Third World countries are, in reality, granted to foreigners – which is to say to subsidiaries of the transnationals (TNCs). Even worse, only about 10 per cent of the patents granted are actually used – but so long as they are in force, no one else can use them. The function of the patent system is to *prevent* the generalization of technology developing in the non-industrialized world.

Susan George, *Ill Fares the Land*

What, then, does Northern technology give to developing nations? First, it is *non-integrated*; that is, its inputs (with the exception of labour) and profits are channelled through foreign companies. Hence, it is not 'transferred', but simply bought and sold. Second, it is usually labour-displacing in countries where unemployment, particularly without a welfare 'safety net', is the number one problem. Third, it leads to regional inequalities and greater emphasis on urban development. Fourth, and most important of all, it replicates and intensifies social and personal injustices in wealth and privilege, the very ground on which any genuine 'development' will ultimately perish.

Decentralized, labour-intensive technology can for many countries, including some in the North, be an appropriate choice. This is not to say that small is beautiful or, indeed, to suggest a return to 'simple', self-contained technology. In the case of agriculture, crop diversity and protection aimed at sustaining a balanced ecosystem would be infinitely more sophisticated than anything on offer at present. Neither should scientific innovation be dismissed out of hand; there is nothing wrong with technology *per se*, provided it is accessible and affordable to all.[6]

The Global Dimension

It is a truism to say we live in a small world. In the North, self-containment is neither possible, nor economically feasible, at a time when even our basic diet comprises items produced in countries that themselves have a serious food problem. The industrial nations are, in spite of popular conceptions to the contrary, the major *importers* of food in world trade; more than two-thirds of all agricultural commodities are directed towards a handful of Northern countries.

Because the dominant industrial food system lends itself to increasing specialization, US and European food surpluses are of particular commodities: wheat, maize, dairy products and (more recently) sugar. By no means is there a deficit of these products in the South, except in exceptional famine situations – and even then, buffer stock arrangements could pre-empt periodic shortfalls. So how do we explain pervasive, crippling hunger in a climate of abundance and overproduction? Frances Moore Lappé:

> If the cause of hunger is neither scarcity of food, nor scarcity of land, we've come to see that it's a scarcity of democracy. That may sound rather contrived, because in the West we tend to think of democracy as a political concept and not as an economic concept. But democracy is really a principle of accountability; in other words, those making the decisions must be accountable to those who are affected by them. Once we understand hunger as a scarcity of democracy, what we are are saying is that from the village level to the level of international commerce, fewer and fewer people are making decisions, and more and more anti-democratic structures are being entrenched. This is the cause of hunger.

We began our investigation into what fuels the hunger machine with the single observation that chronic malnutrition in the world today is a question of injustice. Who could argue with such a basic precept? More importantly, though, we must look for viable alternatives, drawing lessons from proven examples of relative prosperity in the face of overwhelming odds. China, the most densely populated country in the world, managed betwen 1950 and 1980 to reduce its infant mortality rate from 125 to 44 per thousand.

The country created an economic and social miracle that, in the 1930s, was thought unimaginable. Land reform, grain-rationing, sophisticated health care systems, and extended agricultural credit to peasants, have enabled over 1 billion people to stave off hunger and abject poverty, in spite of a per capita income equal to that of some of the poorest countries in the world.

There are other examples: since the 1979 revolution in Nicaragua, the Sandinistas have reduced infant mortality from 120 to less than 80 per thousand, reduced illiteracy from 50 to 10 per cent, and have distributed land to tens of thousands of peasants. Had it not been for the fact that 40 per cent of the national budget has to be spent on defence against the US-backed Contras, even more changes might have occurred. Again, in Tigray and Eritrea, the worst-hit areas of the drought-stricken Horn of Africa, land reform, agricultural innovations and political reform in the rebel-held regions make a profound impact on people's lives. In spite of – even *because* of – decades of bitter warfare, rigorous self-sufficiency is beginning to reap handsome rewards.

What lessons can we draw from such successes? The first, perhaps, is that in an era of US-Soviet political and economic hegemony, there may, in some cases, be no alternative to blood, sweat and tears in paving the way towards radical social change. By 1986, the nations of the world were spending about US$1 million a minute on their military establishments, with an average growth rate of 2.5 per cent per year. When such a huge proportion of this money is used as a vehicle for superpower foreign policy, the efforts of farmers in China, Nicaragua, or Tigray seem a drop in the ocean. But they do provide pointers for the most fundamental changes that must take place if we are to devise a viable long-term strategy against hunger. In these small corners of the globe, power has been vested in the producers, and with that power comes an element of choice, an ability to utilize local productive skills to the benefit of whole communities. Some improvements took place in the context of revolution, others did not. But a common thread ran throughout: ordinary people were given, if only momentarily, the political space within which to create an alternative.

In Minnesota, the Benson family struggle against the odds to run their small, diversified farm. Surveying the awesome changes that have taken place in only one generation, David Benson is apprehensive, but determined:

We need to take extra care with what we're doing here; we must begin to take the long view. Treating it just as a business, as a means of making a dollar, should be only one of a whole galaxy of values, not the driving one which runs the whole show. There's a lot of ordinary folk like us in the world, trying to do just the same. If you look back in history, at civilizations that have prospered, you see that they took that long view. I don't know where we are in the history of this civilization, but all this is rather frightening to me in some ways.

Shaking the dust from his coat, he slowly walks back to his field, to put another season's promise in the ground.

Conclusion: What We Can Do

SUSAN GEORGE

It is said that there are three kinds of people: those who make things happen, those who watch things happen, and those who never knew what hit them. Most of us, presumably, would rather belong to the first category. In the specific case of the hunger crisis, we'd like to make it go away. Fewer and fewer of us can tolerate just watching things happen – like children starving to death on television in living, so to speak, colour. The mail I receive and the audiences I speak to bear witness to the anger and frustration people feel that yet another horrendous famine should strike without apparent warning. (Actually, there is usually plenty of warning, but more about that in a moment.)

Opinion surveys in many countries, especially among the young, show that hunger ranks right at the top, alongside the danger of nuclear war, on their list of the world's most pressing problems. People everywhere, young or old, have had enough of not knowing 'what hit them'; they are asking pointedly why governments and others in authority have done nothing to end hunger and they want to know how they can help stop it.

How indeed can we, the relatively rich, the relatively well-fed, become active members of category number one, and start making things happen? Since you have this book in your hands you've already taken the first and indispensable step: you are making an effort to find out what's actually going on.

Scratch the surface of the hunger issue, and you'll discover that there is a great deal at stake – such as the power and profits of rich and influential minorities in both the North and the South. And, as always when much is at stake, a lot of lies are churned out. This is one reason you've probably heard up to now that hunger is 'caused' by bad weather or by overpopulation, or perhaps exists because the people concerned are lazy or inefficient and don't have the right kind of education and technology. Such explanations are, at best, marginal and deal with aggravating factors, not root causes. This book, and other reading you can undertake (see Appendix 1 on page 223 for some titles) should go a long way towards helping you dispel the myths and disperse the smokescreens.

Self-education (and the education of others) is not some sort of academic exercise. When analysis is wrong, the action that follows it will be necessarily ineffectual or, worse still, harmful to the very people one wants to help. Although most of us start from our emotions – from a moral or religious sense of sheer horror at mass suffering – such emotion is clearly not enough, however necessary as a motivation. Let's assume you agree and want to keep on learning. Then what?

Here are two propositions – the first may sound cynical and the second Pollyanna-ish – but I submit that both are true and a good basis for action.

1 Hungry people, because they are poor are, by definition, of negligible economic interest and limited political clout. Elites, therefore, pay attention to them only when they look like becoming dangerous and upsetting the status quo. It is futile to expect these same elites will take the lead in ridding the world of hunger, unless they believe that they have a positive interest in doing so.

2 As a consequence of (1), 'ordinary' people *can* make a difference – in fact, they are ultimately the only ones who will!

To fight hunger, we must think both tactically and strategically. Tactics means choosing one's strong card and not trying to take on *every* aspect of the stuggle – this is a good recipe for discouragement and for failure. Strategy means knowing where and how to apply pressure, and *to what end*. It means, again, remembering that 'decision-makers' such as high-up politicians, commercial and financial leaders, top personnel in national and international aid agencies, are unlikely to supply those of us lower down with a correct analysis of hunger, let alone effective solutions. If they did, they would be obliged to call their past policies and actions into question, admit that they were wrong, and endanger their privileged positions and interests.

These interests of 'decision-makers' rarely coincide with those of

the poor, because eliminating hunger requires not so much a transfer
of food as a transfer of *power*. This, in turn, implies that we who want
to fight hunger must supply *our own* analysis and invent *our own*
solutions. We must, above all, have confidence that we are capable
of doing this. Solutions will necessarily include a political dimension
because hunger is not just an economic but a political issue. As
Frances Moore Lappé of the Institute for Food and Development
Policy in the USA says, 'There's no scarcity of food. There *is* a
scarcity of democracy.' That statement goes for both the North and
the South, and our task is to promote greater economic and political
democracy wherever and however we can.

Until recently, most (so-called) anti-hunger strategies were
designed by elites in the North for application by elites in the South.
We'll call these elites the 'centres' of power – political, economic and
social. The huge, often destructive 'development' projects, the
food-aid schemes, the 'Green Revolutions' were all decided upon
and put into practice by these 'centres' of power. On the whole, they
have made the plight of the poor worse. Hungry people, in contrast,
live on the 'peripheries' of their societies – they are not 'decision-
makers'. Most of us in the North also inhabit the 'peripheries' of our
own societies, though in rich, democratic countries we have more of
a say than most people living in the South, who may be ill, poorly
organized, and illiterate and who all too often live under single-party
and/or repressive regimes.

Figure 12 shows a way to visualize these relationships. The first
set of circles roughly indicates the way the world is (each circle
would ideally need many sub-components); the second is a vision of
what we should try to make the world. In the North, as I see it, we
should adopt two major strategic goals:

1 Put our own 'centres' under such pressure that they will be
   obliged to adopt policies designed to benefit poor and hungry
   majorities, not just other elites. This is not an impossible
   dream; some countries (in Scandinavia, Holland and to some
   extent, Canada) already practice enlightened development
   cooperation policies, though there is still room for
   improvement.
2 Establish more *direct* links with communities vulnerable to
   hunger. The benefits these people-to-people links confer on
   such communities will make them stronger and put them in a

better position to deal with their own centres, in accordance with their own interests. We cannot do this in their stead. Private voluntary agencies – non-governmental organizations (NGOs) – have lots of valuable experience in the area of people-to-people cooperation, but one can also undertake cooperative ventures from other bases. (Addresses for some NGOs will be found in Appendix 2 on page 225.)

The first rule of thumb is to start from where you are. The genius of a man like Bob Geldof was to ask himself, 'What am I?' Answer: a rock star, who knows other rock stars, who can get together and do

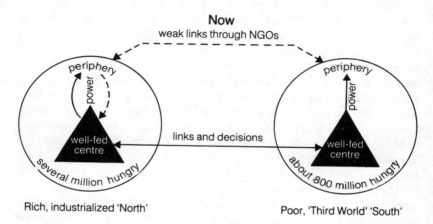

Figure 12

something. But you don't have to be a celebrity and organize the biggest concert in history, everyone belongs to something – a woman's association, a youth or sports club, a civic or professional group, a parish, a school or university, a trade union, a political party, or simply a family, a workplace, town or village. Everyone can become an actor in the struggle against hunger, and even though individual motivation and conviction are indispensable, it's far better to work as part of a group than all alone.

Now let's get down to brass tactics. What do we want from our 'centres', and how might we get it? How does one go about creating or strengthening ties with people who are vulnerable to hunger?

Leaning on the Centre

In most Northern countries, when the time to adopt the annual budget comes round, the development cooperation fund is greeted with a collective yawn – from the left, right and centre. Parliamentarians of every persuasion seize the opportunity to desert the floor. Several (from EEC countries) have told me outright, 'You don't win votes on Third World issues.' We have to convince them they can *lose* votes, in fact ours, on precisely such issues, that we *care* what happens to our tax money.

At present, overseas development budgets are frequently geared more to the needs of the donors than of the recipients. 'Aid' is 'tied', meaning that sums received by Third World country X must be spent in donor country Y. For example, 75 per cent of British bilateral aid is 'tied' to purchases in Britain.

Even if we take tied aid to be a fact of life, we could *at least* insist that our governments approach it in a better way. Instead of deciding what British (or German or Canadian) products *they* want to make Third World countries buy off us, our aid bureaucracies should start from the needs of the poor in partner countries and then see what companies in the donor country could satisfy them. The present system is the equivalent of saying 'We've got the medicine, therefore you've got the disease.'

Although it is a vexed question and makes donors and recipients, alike, extremely nervous, I believe it's high time we placed *conditions* on bilateral (government to government) and multilateral (international agency to government) aid. Such conditions might concern respect for human rights in blatantly repressive countries; more frequently, we should simply be working to make sure that aid reaches the poor people who need it most. While this doesn't mean dictating to recipient states, it does mean being firm about what one wants for one's money. Governments that do not, left to themselves, give their own poor people priority, should not be given discretionary power over aid funds. If our own governments knew they had to satisfy public opinion at home on this count, it would concentrate their minds wonderfully. It would also give them a better bargaining position for taking up the needs of the poor in negotiations with aid partners.

Aid funds for cash crops should, for example, be limited to cases where one is virtually sure they will bring a decent return (e.g. by guaranteeing our own purchases at a mutually determined price, perhaps on a quota system) and that those who do the actual work – the peasantry – will get their fair share.

Since 90 per cent of the people presently going hungry live in the countryside, something approaching that proportion of aid should be going to *rural* development. Village schools, primary health care centres, and measures to improve agriculture, such as farm credit, irrigation and the like, deserve our support far more than the urban projects Third World governments love so well. Urban, aid-financed amenities serve the governments and their city-based political clientèle, not the poor. The only country now giving nearly half its bilateral aid to agriculture, broadly defined, is Denmark. Britain gives a miserly 8 per cent. Donors *could* insist on the right priorities – overwhelmingly *rural* ones – or abstain, but it is up to us to insist that they do so.

We must resist, at all costs, the temptation to dump our own agricultural surpluses on Third World countries, conveniently labelling them 'food aid', except in times of real emergency need. Most people believe that food aid *is* emergency aid. Not so, only about 10 per cent of it, even in times of famine, serves to alleviate natural or man-made disasters. The rest is programmed year in, year out, no matter what the local food situation. Some powerful lobbies in the North are anxious to hide a shattering fact: food aid can, and does, *contribute* to hunger.

Imagine you are a farmer somewhere in the Third World, just getting by. This year, you've had a bumper crop and are blessing heaven as you take it to market. When you get there, you learn that shiploads of EEC or US grain have just arrived, with more promised. The price you expected to receive for your own crop does a nosedive; you have been effectively placed in competition with free, or abnormally cheap, subsidized food from Iowa or East Anglia. Your own family's consumption is going to suffer, you will have little or nothing left to invest in next year's crop. If you were already living close to the brink, you may not be able to pay off your debts and may have to cash in your animals or even sell off your land.

This is not a fantasy scenario. It has occurred countless times in 'aided' countries. Inappropriate food aid thus feeds itself, by destroying the livelihoods of farmers on the spot. When they can no longer make a living in the countryside, they and their families will end up emigrating to the cities, where they may well require food aid. . .

Food aid also changes local eating habits, particularly those of urban residents towards whom governments direct most of the hand-outs from abroad. People learn to like the taste and convenience of bread, never mind that wheat won't grow in their country. They also learn to scorn local grains like sorghum or millet as 'inferior', further reducing the market for their own farmers and reinforcing their dependency on outside suppliers. Food exporting countries, in fact, count on just such reactions. They make no bones about the fact that free (or very cheap) food today should lead to cash sales tomorrow. In the time-worn phrase of the US 'Food for Peace' programme, recipient countries should move from 'aid to trade'.

Searing images of the African famine are still fresh in our memories. Surely food aid is amply justified in such cases? Obviously when things have come to such a pass, we are morally bound to send food. But hunger crises are avoidable, and this is something else we've got to hammer into our governments' thick heads. Famines are like cancers: they take months, even years, to build up to a life-threatening crisis. As with cancers, there are plenty of warning signs which anyone with two eyes, two feet and a checklist can learn to recognize. You do not need satellite photography and computers to check out the state of the crops (though flashy technology may help to convince governments that a famine prevention campaign is urgent).

The British colonial administration in India devised a perfectly usable famine-warning checklist. Their local officers were expected to note tell-tale rural phenomena that still signal danger today. A famine is undoubtedly looming if enough of the following signs are present:

1 grain prices are rising (due to real shortages or hoarding);
2 animal prices are falling (because of mass cash sales to buy food);
3 women are seeking 'famine foods' not eaten in normal times, or selling their jewelry and utensils;
4 men are migrating further and further out in search of work;
5 unusual numbers of beggars, especially children, are going from house to house;
6 wages are declining, or are paid only in kind;
7 the value of land is depreciating as more people try to sell their last assets.

More often than not, there is *plenty of food* around in famine times. But poor people simply do not have access to it, while speculators and hoarders make fortunes. A famine is not a disaster for everyone! By ignoring the warning signs, by allowing a minor shortage to bloom and flourish and become a full-blown disaster, we ensure not only that substantial numbers of people will die, but that the survivors will be worse-off than before. How could it be otherwise, when people have eaten their seed grain, sold off their farm implements and their animals and, sometimes, their land?

The first duty of an aid programme worthy of the name is to *help people stay in their own villages*. A famine camp, like the ones we have all seen on television, is where people unwillingly go as a last resort when both they and their resources are totally exhausted. It is not just 'the closest thing to hell on earth'; it is graphic proof of our collective failure.

Can one always help famine victims through their governments? Many observers and practitioners will disagree, but I fear there are cases when one must, at whatever diplomatic cost, work only through NGOs. Governments that turn against their own people and consciously deny them food are not to be trusted, or helped. In the recent past, the government of Ethiopia has tried to 'starve out' the rebels in the northern, secessionist provinces of Tigray and Eritrea, going so far as to bomb fleeing columns of refugees and fields about to be harvested.

The imperial past and present politics of Ethiopia are too complex to relate here, but were the matter left to me, I would work with the Relief Society of Tigray (REST) and the Eritrean Relief Association (ERA), even if it meant being ostracized by the central government. At the very least, private aid can be channelled through such organizations (addresses in Appendix 2).

Here's an experimental 'what-to-do' idea of which I'm not altogether confident. Who wants to improve on it and lobby for it? Third World countries are spending more and more on arms and armies, which are totally unproductive, while direly needed investment in health, agriculture, education, and the like, gets short shrift. Couldn't the rich countries, individually or collectively, propose 'security pacts' to selected Third World countries, promising them help in the form of arbitration or even intervention in case of attack, in exchange for a reduction in military spending and a corresponding shift to financing life-enhancing activities?

Here's another idea of which I'm *totally* confident! We should insist that our governments *protect successful experiments*. Third World governments actually giving pride of place to the interests and livelihoods of poor people are so rare, we should cherish and nurture those that do, instead of thwarting their efforts and, upon occasion, actively fighting against them.

I don't, for example, think the Sandinistas are perfect but I do know, from observation and from impartial sources, that in Nicaragua the infant mortality rate has been dramatically reduced, tens of thousands of previously landless peasants have received legal title to land; and, in so far as the US blockade allows, everyone, including the poorest, gets a basic diet, basic health care and basic education.

Before the Sandinistas came to power Nicaragua was, under Somoza, the worst-fed country in Central America – the *average* ration was around 1,770 calories a day, meaning that the poorest were living at starvation level. Oxfam has called the turnaround in Nicaragua 'the threat of a good example'. We should meditate on this, and oblige our political leaders to do so as well. Another country that has placed much hope in its peasantry is Zimbabwe. Such countries should be supported so that they can consolidate their gains.

In the 1980s, the debt crisis is a new factor forcing hunger and misery upon millions of people. News about it is, however, usually confined to the financial pages, where there is much dithering about what might happen to the banks and to the international financial system if major debtors cannot pay up. Little or no space is devoted to those who are actually called upon to make sacrifices so that their governments can reimburse foreign debts. A joke circulating in Latin America puts it better than I can: *Official to citizen:* 'You'll have to tighten your belt.' *Citizen to official:* 'I can't. I ate it yesterday.'

Many debts will have to be forgiven anyway, so why prolong the agony? No one profits from the present situation, except for tiny and privileged minorities (banks in particular). Many job losses in the North can be directly ascribed to the debt owed by the South – countries are so overburdened they simply cannot afford to buy anything we produce. Writing off debts and lower interest rates would help; but even debt, used creatively, could become an instrument for promoting democracy.

Why not let countries pay back part of their debt, *in their own currencies*, to national or regional development funds, to which local groups (women's and peasants' associations, cooperatives, urban slum neighbourhoods, etc.) could then apply for help in undertaking their own projects? For African countries, where most of the debt is public (i.e. not held by private banks, but by Western governments) we could even think about reimbursement in kind. Put a price-tag on, say, reafforestation, or on literacy campaigns or credit programmes for farmers, and let the indebted government mobilize its own resources to do the job. The debt would be reduced by the corresponding amount in exchange for progress on these mutually agreed targets.

About three-quarters of all aid to the Third World is channelled bilaterally, government to government. The remaining 25 per cent goes to international agencies whose records range from the superb to the pretty awful. My own favourites are the International Fund for Agricultural Development (IFAD) and the UN Children's Fund, UNICEF. Everyone knows about UNICEF's work for children; not everyone knows that it gets no regular budget from UN headquarters but must rely on direct contributions from donor governments. Sometimes it happens that the *people* of a country give more to UNICEF (by buying Christmas cards, etc.) than their governments do, as in France where, in 1985, the French gave three and a half times as much as their government contribution of US$3.6 million. The British, on the other hand could do better: their government gave US$8.5 million and British citizens gave only US$2.2 million in 1985.

IFAD is less well known, and is younger but, as its name indicates, this fund is entirely dedicated to improving the situation of the rural poor and has done highly innovative work in reaching small farmers with credit and technical expertise or promoting a better deal for rural women, for example. Financed both by OPEC and Western countries, IFAD has had to suffer through endless haggling between them at each 'replenishment' of its funds. The USA has lately dragged its feet in a particularly offensive way and dragged a lot of its allies along as well. Consequently, IFAD now has much less money to work with, even though its cost-effectiveness is demonstrably higher than that of most other agencies. This is scandalous, and the sooner citizens find out about IFAD and help it forward, the better.

This may seem a daunting list of tasks, and in many ways it is. How can the mythical 'ordinary' person help to get results? RESULTS is precisely the name of a US anti-hunger citizens' lobbying group that could become a model for any other parliamentary democracy. The idea is simply that members communicate their concern about world (or American) hunger to their elected representatives, in a systematic way.

Local US RESULTS groups pick the hunger issues (usually with assistance from the national office), learn to communicate the basic facts about them and generate letters and telephone calls to members of Congress, as well as briefings when members return to their home districts. Suddenly the Congressperson from Austin, Texas or Hartford, Connecticut, discovers that his constituents not only know what IFAD is, but expect him to do something about it. Debates are launched in local media; hunger issues become community issues. Founded in 1980, there are now over 50 RESULTS groups in 30 states and a national office in Washington, which coordinates lobbying efforts. RESULTS is entirely financed by private contributions, usually by people who subscribe a monthly sum.

Getting money for new social expenditure from the Reagan Administration has been notoriously hard, but RESULTS helped to obtain US$50 million for a good cause. As a member of the House Select Committee on Hunger wrote: 'The work of RESULTS participants on the Global Primary Health Care Initiative was truly extraordinary and demonstrated that concerned and motivated

citizens really can have a successful impact on the legislative process
. . . The RESULTS work was citizen lobbying at its best . . . We
couldn't have done it without you!'[1] RESULTS itself simply says it
is a 'nationwide, grass-roots citizen's lobby dedicated to the
knowledge that each one of us *does* make a difference.' And that is
what counts – to believe that one can make a difference.

Another organization, this one European, has also had some
success. Food and Disarmament International (FDI) has put
pressure on governments, notably in Italy and Belgium, to increase
their development cooperation budgets and to give priority to Third
World regions where the greatest number of lives are at risk from
malnutrition and starvation. FDI has been able to mobilize large
numbers of people for marches, lobbying and the like; it also
concentrates on getting backing from local government officials and
other politicians. At its behest, close to 100 Nobel Prizewinners have
got behind its manifesto against hunger.

The drawback to FDI is, however, like many such organizations,
it is understaffed and underfunded and cannot put as much energy
into overseeing how the money is actually spent as it does on
mobilizing the money in the first place. Thanks to pressure from
FDI and its friends, the Italian aid budget has quadrupled in just a
few years. But the Italian bureaucracy has given birth to a
two-headed monster for dispensing the funds – one for 'emergencies'
and another, quite separate one, for 'development'. Since emergencies occur, and will continue to occur because development has
failed, it is not only wasteful but foolish to pretend they can be kept
apart by administrative fiat. In Belgium, it is as yet unclear how
much new money has really been allocated to hard-hit areas as a
result of a new FDI-inspired law, and how much merely transferred
from other budget pigeon-holes. As the FDI case shows, thinking
strategically also means knowing what further practical steps to take
if one scores a victory, and how to sustain momentum in the right
direction.

Unfortunately, there's no substitute for pushing our governments
to pay more attention to Third World needs. They will not do so
spontaneously and they will not usually remain concerned for long.
If eternal vigilance is the price of freedom, it is also the price of a
decent and humane development cooperation policy. Remember
that, without the outcry of public opinion, nearly all Western
governments would have turned their backs on Cambodia during

the famine of the late 1970s and, more recently, would have left Africa to its fate. Cambodia was occupied by a political adversary, Vietnam, which the West did not want to aid in any way, no matter how many people were starving; Africa represents only a tiny percentage of world trade and investment and is, thus, of scant interest.

Although states are rarely moved by humanitarian impulses, unless forced by their own constituencies, they are, alas, the ones who have the serious money! Even the record sums raised by Bandaid, Sportaid and the like are insignificant compared to what states can afford, if they want to. Development *spending*, however, does not always automatically equal development – far from it. Fortunately, the amount of money is often less important *than the recipient*. This leads us to our second big 'What to do' heading.

Making People-to-People Connections

As noted above, there are precious few Third World governments that give their poor people, and especially their peasantries, high priority. So we should never confuse countries with citizens, or rulers with people, when we choose our development partners. It's also well to recall that our own governments may often have a positive stake in perpetuating some of the nastier Third World regimes – the very ones who protect 'our' investments and supply 'us' with docile, low-cost labour and cheap raw materials. It is, therefore, most unlikely that our governments will try to strengthen poor majorities against their rulers.

I use quotation marks around 'our' and 'us' because most of us in the North gain little or nothing from continuing poverty and repression in the South. Quite the contrary: we positively lose from these inequalities. As long as the Third World work-force is oppressed and underpaid, joblessness and downward pressure on wages will increase for us too, as transnational corporations move many of their operations abroad, or maintain an unfair advantage over national enterprises that cannot compete on the same terms. Until workers, wherever they live, are paid approximately the same wages for the same day's work, plants in the North will continue to close because, however great their productivity, they cannot compete against sweat-shops in the South.

Nor do we even gain, except in the odd case, from cheap raw materials, though some of our corporations may. Value is added to these primary products by our own firms. Activities like processing, packaging, storage, distribution and advertising (and the comfortable mark-ups that go with them) determine prices for finished goods of which raw materials are a relatively small component. Have you noticed, for example, the price of a chocolate bar going down? No? How odd, since prices for sugar and cocoa beans have been steadily dwindling.

In other words, when we help poor communities in the Third World gain more control over the circumstances of their own lives, we are not only acting in their interests *but in our own as well.* Healthier economies in the South, which only well-fed, decently paid people can sustain, will create greater prosperity in the North; not least because they will want to buy what we produce.

If this is the case, why don't our governments and our commercial and financial leaders do everything in their power to promote healthier and more democratic Third World economies? Part of the answer is that the time-scale they work to is incredibly limited. Take a close look at the debt crisis and you will soon arrive at the conclusion that for an international banker, three months is a very long time. He cannot comprehend that he is killing the golden goose (and quite possibly his own bank) when he demands, for example, that Latin American countries make net transfers to the North of over US$100 billion dollars, as they did between 1982 and 1985. Don't ask the banker to plan in terms of a few years – for him a period bordering on eternity – just as it is fruitless to ask most corporate managers to look beyond their 12-month profit and loss statement.

Government aid bureaucracies may change personnel with every shift in the political wind and they, too, have 12-month budgets. Anything unspent this year means less next – so the rule is to get rid of the money, never mind whether it helps or harms the poor. Most Northern governments are not *interested* in the problems of the Third World, except as these may have a bearing on their own problems, and govern largely on behalf of a privileged minority at home; often they simply don't know what they're doing.

Uncritically aping the methodologies prescribed by bodies like the IMF or the World Bank, Northern governments make the same mistakes over and over again, at the expense of countless millions of poor and hungry people. It takes a first class catastrophe – probably something even worse than the recent famine in Africa – to make them re-examine their methods, much less their goals.

You may disagree and believe we can safely leave Third World problems to our own 'centres'; or, if you agree, you may find the present state of affairs appalling. It is, but it can also be liberating for each of us to realize that if those in authority don't know what they're doing, and care less, then *it is up to us*. We must somehow try to make up for their incompetence, their stubbornness or their hostility towards the poor.

To get a feel for people-to-people connections, and for what real development is all about, I would strongly recommend first joining a local group of one of the non-governmental organizations. These NGOs have been in the field for years, and they have invaluable experience concerning what works and what doesn't. They know who's who in the Third World and they organize anti-hunger campaigns that are aimed at educating public opinion at home as well as fundraising (e.g. Oxfam's 'Hungry for Change' campaign, or the Catholic Fund for Overseas Development – Cafod's – campaign on 'Just Food'). You can become an activist in such campaigns or, failing that, simply send a contribution and familiarize yourself with the literature.

Once you have a sense of the pitfalls to avoid, if you want a sense of personal involvement and solidarity, you can start a project with a Third World partner from nearly any base – any group you belong to that is similarly inclined or that you can convince of the need to act. In France, where I live, I know of dozens of such groups. Usually they begin because someone took a cheap charter on holiday to Burkina Faso and met some local people and they started talking . . .or the cousin of one of the village municipal counsellors is a teacher near Bamako and she wrote about how much a well could improve the lives of the people in her village. . .or student volunteers went to help build a dispensary in Nicaragua over the summer and came back full of enthusiasm. . .or two priests, from France and Africa, met at a theology congress and started talking about the problems in their respective parishes.

The stories are all different, but the gist is the same. Somewhere in a poor country, ordinary people have identified a *need*. Somewhere in a developed country, a group has decided that it wants to contribute to human solidarity and justice. The need identified by the Third World group may seem to have only an indirect connection with hunger, malnutrition and poverty, but this is their prerogative. One Latin American peasant group decided, for example, that their greatest need was for a small lorry and training in mechanics to keep it running. Why? Because they were totally dependent on middle-men who came to the village and underpaid their produce. With a lorry, they could get the produce to market in town themselves, and make a lot more money, some of which, we can assume, would be spent on better food for the people.

In other words, people in the South know their situation better than we do. Just be careful that the person proposing the project is not an 'operator' – there are some who have learned how to manipulate the generosity of outsiders for private gain. Usually, it's best to work with an already functioning group – of women peasants, for example. One must, above all, be sure that the project will benefit everyone, as equally as possible, including the worst-off people. Villages have their own power structures, and there's nothing worse than increasing the capacity of the local elite to sabotage the efforts of the poor. Projects should be designed to become *self-sustaining* after a mutually determined period. The point of people-to-people aid is to make oneself redundant, to create self-reliance as well as greater material assets.

When in doubt, or if you don't know any group you can support, ask the help of one of the experienced NGOs. They may have more good project proposals than they can finance themselves. In France, at least, associations of immigrant workers are also good sources of projects – they are themselves helping their home villages. Churches are also excellent channels, especially in countries where they may be among the few institutions allowed to operate freely.

One of my favourite project stories is about eight Swiss housewives who learned of the appalling conditions on banana plantations in Guatemala. They got local supermarkets to propose a small mark-up on bananas (to those who accepted it – it wasn't compulsory), they provided educational materials for the customers, and the stores turned over the difference to the women, who in turn channelled the money to the association of plantation workers in Guatemala, through a church organization.

How are you to finance your chosen project? This depends on your imagination, as the Swiss example shows. There are, of course, the traditional bake and jumble sales. Some small towns that have decided to 'twin' themselves with Third World communities have added a few pennies to the rates for water (again, people can specifically refuse to pay, but usually they don't). This creates a small fund for sustaining the project undertaken by the community as a whole.

I'm often asked 'life-style' questions – most frequently, 'Shall I eat less (or no) meat?' because animals consume a lot of grain, which we then consume as meat. I'm not a vegetarian myself, and this perhaps colours my response, but I truly believe that economic systems are able to adjust all too easily to such choices. The world is presently awash with grain – but poor people cannot afford it *at any price*. Adding to the stockpile, is not, it seems to me, going to do any good. However, if you decide consciously to fast (or do without something else) in order to contribute the price of the steak or chop or material object to a development NGO, that is an entirely different matter. Voluntary acts of this nature keep us in good moral (and physical) tone, but one should harbour no illusions as to their *economic* impact.

An exception is the consumer boycott, like the one carried out against Nestlé on the issue of baby milk marketing in poor countries. Though the company kept insisting the boycott did not harm its sales, it certainly kept them from *growing* as much as Nestlé had hoped, and brought a deluge of unfavourable publicity. Whatever Nestlé claimed, the fact remains that the company did eventually stop pushing infant formula in places where mothers could neither afford it nor prepare it hygienically. In such cases, your consumer choices can definitely contribute to desirable change.

In a general way, consumer issues should be judged on three basic criteria (which I borrow here from the Berne Declaration Group in Switzerland): *health, ecology, justice*. Does the product damage your health (or that of the producer and/or processor)? Did producing it contribute to pollution of the environment or draw excessively on non-renewable resources? Did the producer (as far as one can know) receive a decent return for his/her labour? If consumer groups could ask themselves such questions, and move their thinking from *products* (comparing five brands of instant coffee) to the *process* that put this product in our cupboards, they would take an important step forward. Supermarket shopping could become an exercise in consciousness raising!

People frequently ask me in hushed and confidential tones, 'Do you *really* believe we can get rid of hunger? Isn't it utopian to pretend we can?' My answer is 'Yes, I really do believe we can' and

'Yes, it is utopian.'

Is this a contradiction in terms? Only for those with no sense of history. A century and a half ago, it was utopian to believe one could rid the USA of slavery. The divine right of kings once seemed far more firmly entrenched than the tyrannies that are common coin in the Third World today. Another fratricidal war between Western European nations is now as implausible as one between the USA and Canada. Millions of people are still around who can give a first-hand account of intra-Western slaughter in the First and Second World Wars. Ask them whether a peaceful Europe seemed possible 50 years ago.

Ask, for that matter, the average Chinese peasant how well his father and mother fared. Not for nothing was the Chinese version of 'Hello, how are you?' or *'Comment ça va?'*, 'Have you eaten?' The point is that hunger has *already* been eliminated over huge areas, and for huge populations. If it were a *natural* phenomenon, there would be true cause for despair and I, for one, would be in a different line of work. But if, as I hope this book has convinced you, hunger is a *political* and *economic* phenomenon, then there are no excuses for its persistence.

A sense of history is vital. The powerful and the privileged, wherever they live, have always claimed that any change in the status quo would bring civilization as we know it to a dead halt. Somehow, civilization has survived. We, who are now among the well-fed, have not only moral obligations to the hungry in the present, but to our own past as well. We have debts to those who came before us, to the workers and farmers, the women and minorities, to all those who fought for justice in our own countries. Their struggles changed the context in which we are now privileged to live; they fought for our own right to fight. Many of them suffered from hunger too. Thanks to them, we can speak out and we can act without fear of reprisal. The battlefields may be different; the vision is the same one that has always inspired change. Thanks to the vision of those who came before us, yesterday's utopias are nearer now. Today's are our responsibility to the future.

Many people still wonder, however, whether the elimination of hunger can be attained only by accepting a certain loss of freedom. Countries like China have made great strides, true, but at what human cost? Coercion, authoritarianism, imprisonment, even death have also been part of the success stories of some nations that have reduced or conquered hunger. Must one choose between the right to food and other human rights?

Definitely not: I repeat that the goal will be ultimately attained through *greater economic and political democracy* in the First World and the Third. But we must be clear about what we mean by 'human rights' and 'freedom'. The standard international legal instruments recognize two kinds of human rights and these, unfortunately, have often been kept separate for political reasons.

The first set are the civil and political rights such as freedom of speech, of assembly, of worship; the right not to be deprived of liberty or tortured or killed because of one's beliefs, race or gender. The international covenants setting out these civil and political rights have generally been ratified by the Western countries. These same countries have not, however, always accepted the covenants on economic, social and cultural rights that socialist countries see as more important.

The right to food figures specifically in both these sets of rights, because without the food that sustains life, all other rights would be meaningless. If we accept the full scope of human rights, we must work for a world in which civil and political, economic, social and cultural rights are seen as equally important. Obstacles to be surmounted on this road include the downgrading of *individual* rights by socialist countries and the parallel refusal of capitalist countries to accept the notion of *collective* rights.

Indeed, the elites of our own capitalist countries tend to equate freedom simply with the 'free' market. Only a singular distortion of language – and a triumph of ideology – allows us to call anything so utterly rigged 'free'. Might makes right: for dozens of countries, the market ensures permanent poverty, because it refuses to pay a fair price for their products and their labour. For millions of poor people, an unfettered market conveys only the freedom to starve. Remarks about the freedom of the fox and that of the chickens, that of the lion as compared to the lamb, are not without pertinence. As Woody Allen says, 'The lion may lie down with the lamb, but the lamb isn't going to get a lot of sleep.'

Without making a case for feudalism or paternalism, it's still relevant to point out that these 'archaic' or 'primitive' systems did provide some safety nets for the poor, if only because the powerful could not afford to let them starve. People had grazing or gleaning rights, they could gather free firewood and building materials, they had a right to some food from the landlords' stores in times of scarcity, or to a small piece of land for their own use. In many societies, the suggestion that land could be sold or alienated would have been about as acceptable as the idea of selling one's mother. Attempts to rescind these rights sometimes led to revolutions.

Furthermore, in times past, a community or a state was *defined* by who had a right to eat and who didn't. Food was the basic necessity through which you knew what group you belonged to and where the boundaries were. Think of 'bread and circuses': *panem*, like *circenses*, were due to Romans, but not to outsiders. Medieval towns in Britain had a responsiblity for the subsistence of anyone born within their confines until that person came of age. The Chinese empires had elaborate mechanisms and chains of command for keeping 'ever-normal' granaries and coping with shortage. African custom decreed sharing of resources, particularly of food and land. Because of low productivity, because of warfare or civil strife, these systems could and did break down, but safety nets for the weaker members of the community were the recognized social *norm* even if they were not always respected and often didn't work.

Most of these support systems have now been swept aside by untrammeled 'free' markets. The basic necessities of life (including food), land, even people have become nothing but commodities. Capitalism has been an unparalleled creator of wealth but has put nothing in the place of the customary safety nets it has destroyed, except where *political* struggle has obliged it to do so. For the past couple of centuries, much of Western politics has been about precisely this question, not yet resolved: how to keep the market functioning without unacceptable social casualties. If this question had been settled, several million American citizens would not be going hungry today.

One lesson of experience is clear: the 'market', left to its own devices, is never going to feed everybody. Even in these times of comparatively low grain prices and monster food stocks, millions are still too poor to buy them. In this sense, we need a work revolution as much as a food and land revolution. So long as people cannot grow their food or earn the wages to buy it, hunger will remain. Behind hunger lies poverty; behind poverty lie inequality and the market's incapacity to satisfy peoples' right to work. In this 'free' system, hungry people are superfluous people – and vice-versa.

A number of countries, including many in the Third World, have devoted considerable efforts to defining 'poverty lines'. Needless to say, they have not set their statisticians and economists the task of defining corresponding wealth lines. When people fall below the poverty line, they have no net, so they drop into oblivion. Death is the lower limit. There is no upper limit. In Brazil, the income differential between the richest and the poorest is now measured by a factor of several hundred.

Is it completely insane to think that one day we might democratically determine wealth lines? (To a certain extent, that's what taxes are. Very few Third World countries even have income taxes, or could collect them if they had.) Is it wild to suggest that we might tax sales of arms and other lethal products in the North to provide development funds for the South; that international financial settlements might be based on the composite price of a basket of commodities so that the Third World would not be penalized every time the dollar or interest rates fluctuated? Ideas are not lacking, but when the concept of 'freedom' is bastardized to the point that it becomes the 'freedom' of unlimited accumulation by an individual, a corporation or, for that matter, a nation or group of nations at the expense of others' survival, something is deeply wrong with our system.

If one lacks the unbounded faith of Reagan or Thatcher in the market to eliminate hunger, does this mean that one should espouse rigid, centralized, planning as the salvation of millions of poverty-stricken, hungry people? Not in my view. Such systems have not worked to date and show no signs of doing so in the future, for deep historical reasons related to the very nature of the peasantry. No progress in the Third World is possible without concentration on, and cooperation with, small farmers and landless peasants, particularly women who produce so much of the food.

A pro-peasant, pro-women food security strategy is the opposite of what has passed for 'modernization' up to now. Modernization along Western lines leads to land concentration, loss of employment, and outmigration to cities, whereas the point of a food strategy is to help keep people in the rural areas by improving their chances of a decent livelihood there. This means paying them fairly for what they produce and making sure enough goods and services are available in the countryside to make living there attractive. Markets should be allowed to do what they can do well – encourage individual initiative, create employment, set prices through competition, furnish a decent return on investment. They should not provide a licence for landlords, moneylenders and middlemen to exploit the poor in the name of 'freedom'.

Markets alone will never allocate the necessary resources to the countryside: only governments can do that. Alas, though, instead of helping to ensure peoples' right to food, many states now govern on behalf of the very exploiters who violate this right. In market-economy countries, the rights of property – in unlimited quantities – supersede the right to food. So-called socialist countries may deny any initiative to their own peasantries and, thus, also deprive them of their right to subsistence.

As the human rights scholar Philip Alston has put it,

In the final analysis, appropriate policies will be adopted not as a result of technocratic altruism, but only in response to widespread and insistent popular outrage. For that reason, an emphasis on the role of law must not be permitted to obscure the importance of viewing the concept of the right to food essentially as a mobilizing force, as a rallying point, through which people themselves are encouraged to assert their rights by making use of all appropriate legal and extra-legal means.[2]

Note that Alston specifically cites *extra-legal* means. If we take seriously the right to food for all, we must ask ourselves equally serious questions about justice. Are we prepared to accept that the first right of those deprived of food is to organize resistance against those who violate their rights? Would we stand with the Bishop of Fortaleza in Brazil, who approved a starving mob that stormed a full granary, saying that the right to food is more important than the right to property? Will we confront the forces in our own societies that deprive people of food, even indirectly? The right to food and the freedom to resist injustice are inseparable, because there is no freedom without bread, and no bread without freedom.

Nor is there a shortage of work to be done on the frontlines of hunger. But we shall need our sense of history, because it's going to be a long haul. The worst service one can do to the cause of the hungry is to pretend that everything can be solved in one glorious burst of energy. The nature of *time* is different in our countries and in, say, Africa. We want quick results, whereas Africa is labouring under the burden of a hundred years of colonialism, 30 years of spurious 'development' ruinous for the peasantry and the environment, with 10 years of drought thrown in for good measure. Only those armed with perseverance and patience should get involved in fighting against that kind of legacy.

It worries me that the funds raised by organizations like Oxfam or War on Want should depend on how much coverage notoriously fickle editors (film or print) devote to hunger. When they decide that the public has had enough of the subject, hunger again becomes a non-event, no matter how many people are still quietly dying.

It worries me too that the media have portrayed the hungry almost exclusively as victims, waiting for hand-outs by the side of the road. There they are – inert, apathetic and miserable – apparently waiting for us to come and do something about them. Anyone but a saint would contract a fierce case of 'compassion fatigue' with this steady diet of images of passive and helpless people. Such images may have already captured the imaginations of

a whole generation, who may shut them out next time round and forget them as soon as they humanly can.

The only antidote to compassion fatigue is the truth: for every person pictured in the last extremities of exhaustion, there are a thousand others at work, stuggling to make what they can of their environment with little help from God or man. For every person who can live only by hand-outs, there are a hundred thousand more who ask only to grow their food or to earn the wages to buy it. Hungry and poor people are not beggars nor an aggregate of empty stomachs; they are already at work with their heads and the hands and they have not waited for 'us'. We can become partners, participants in their struggle. We cannot be its leaders, because development is not something that can be done *to* people. But we can take our common humanity seriously and affirm, with the song, that 'We are the World'. So let's start changing it.

References

1 The Creation of Hunger

1 World Bank, *Annual Report 1984*.
2 Julius K. Nyerere, 'A Trade Union for the Poor', *Bulletin of the Atom Sciences* 35 (6), (June 1979), pp. 38, 39.
3 Jan Tinbergen, et al., *Reshaping the International Order: A Report to the Club of Rome* (E. P. Dutton & Co., New York, 1976), p. 28.
4 *Population Misconceptions* (Population Concern, 1984).
5 The Hunger Project, *Ending Hunger* (Praeger, New York, 1985), p. 23.
6 *New Internationalist* (September 1985), p. 25.
7 Unless otherwise attributed, personal interviews such as this were with Jon Bennett or Yorkshire Television.
8 CWDE, *Commodity Sheet 3: Rice* (London, 1983).
9 *North–South: A Programme for Survival*, (The 'Brandt Report'), (Pan, London, 1980), p. 25.
10 Ibid.
11 World Food Conference, 'The Declaration of the Eradication of Hunger and Malnutrition' (1974).
12 US Department of Agriculture, *World Agriculture Supply and Demands Estimates* (WASDE) 193, (9 May 1986).
13 Hunger Project, *Ending Hunger*, p. 129.
14 Cafod, *Just Food* (Cafod, London, 1984), p. 5.
15 J. Hightower, *Eat Your Heart Out: Food Profiteering in America* (Crown, New York, 1975), p. 162.
16 Figures from UNCTAD, cited in Nigel Twose, *Cultivating Hunger* (Oxfam, Oxford, 1984).
17 Anthony Sampson, *The Money Lenders* (Hodder & Stoughton, London, 1981), cited in Twose, *Cultivating Hunger*.
18 CIA, *Potential Implications of Trends in World Population, Food Production and Climate* (CIA, Washington DC, 1974) 2, pp. 40–1, cited in Anne Buchanan, *Food, Poverty & Power* (Spokesman, Nottingham), 1982.

19 Ibid.
20 John Brock, quoted in Bill Rau, *Feast to Famine* (Africa Faith & Justice Network, 1985).

2 Sudan: Fortunes and Famine

1 Sudan Relief and Rehabilitation Commission, *Monthly Report* (RICSU, Khartoum, November 1985).
2 Barbara Dinham and Colin Hines, *Agribusiness in Africa* (Earth Resources Research, London, 1983).
3 Zeinab Bedawi, Research Notes, Yorkshire Television, 1986.
4 Nick Cater, *Sudan: The Roots of Famine* (Oxfam, Oxford, 1986), p. 16.
5 UNHCR, *Profile: Sudan* (UNHCR, Geneva, June 1985).

3 Aid: The Poisoned Gift?

1 World Bank, *World Development Report, 1986*.
2 World Bank, *Annual Report, 1986*.
3 John Clark, *For Richer, For Poorer* (Oxfam, Oxford, 1986).
4 See Frances Moore Lappé and Joseph Collins, *Aid As Obstacle* (Institute for Food & Development Policy, San Francisco, 1980), pp. 39–40.
5 Betsy Hartmann and James Boyce, *Needless Hunger: Voices from a Bangladesh Village* (Institute for Food and Development Policy, San Francisco, 1979), cited in Lappé & Collins, *Aid as Obstacle*, pp. 57–8.
6 Tom Learmouth and Frances Rolt, *Underdeveloping Bangladesh: 225 Years of British Investment* (War on Want, London, 1981), p. 22.
7 World Bank, *World Development Report, 1986*, p. 146.
8 Lappé & Collins, *Aid as Obstacle*, p. 107.
9 World Bank, *Bangladesh: Food Policy Review* (Washington, World Bank, 1977), p. 39, cited in Lappé & Collins, *Aid as Obstacle*, p. 107.
10 Amnesty International, *Annual Report, 1977* (AI Publications, London), pp. 169–73.
11 Overseas Development Administration, *Overseas Development* (London) 73, (October 1981).

4 Losing the Trade Game

1 Nigel Twose, *Cultivating Hunger* (Oxfam, Oxford, 1985), p. 22.
2 André Gunder Frank, *Capitalism and Underdevelopment in Latin America* (Penguin, Harmondsworth, 1971), pp. 311–12.

3 Basil Davidson, *Which Way Africa?* (Penguin, Harmondsworth, 1967), p. 44.
4 *North – South: A Programme for Survival* (The 'Brandt Report'), (Pan, London, 1980), p. 91.
5 Ibid., p. 62.
6 UNCTAD, *Annual Economic Review, 1984*, figures for 1982.
7 World Bank, *Annual Report, 1985*.
8 World Bank, *World Development Report, 1986*.
9 'A World Bank Pipe-Dream', *Financial Times* (8 July 1986).
10 UNCTAD, *Annual Economic Review, 1986*.

5 Brazil: Miracle or Mirage?

1 World Health Organisation statistics, *Annual Report, 1984*.
2 Quoted in Cafod, *Brazil, Basic Facts* (Cafod, London, 1985).
3 Cafod, *Brazil:Basic Facts*.
4 Teresa Hayter and Catherine Watson, *Aid – Rhetoric and Reality* (Pluto Press, London, 1985).
5 World Bank, *World Development Report, 1986*.
6 *Wall Street Journal* (February 1986).
7 A term given to the area by Brazilian President Gertulio Vargas in 1936.
8 A request for support from Cafod, cited in *CAFOD's Development Programme in Brazil, 1984* (Cafod, London, 1984), p. 2.
9 See publications of Survival International, London.
10 Cited in Oxfam Public Affairs Unit, *An Unnatural Disaster: Drought in NE Brazil* (Oxfam, Oxford, 1984).
11 Ibid., p. 10.
12 Roger Burbach and Patricia Flynn, *Agribusiness in the Americas* (Monthly Review Press with NACLA, London, 1980), p. 141.
13 World Bank, *World Development Report, 1986*.
14 Ibid.
15 *Liberate the Land: a Statement by the Bishops of Brazil* (Catholic Institute for International Relations, London, 1986), p. 6.
16 Oxfam nutritional survey, 1985.
17 *Brazil 2000*, commissioned by the Brazilian government.
18 René Dumont, *Lands Alive* (Monthly Review Press, London, 1965), ch. 3.

6 Exporting Recession: The USA Pays the Price

1 Susan George, *Ill Fares the Land* (Institute for Policy Studies, Washington DC, 1984), p. 23.
2 Physician's Task Force on Hunger, 'Hunger in America', (Harvard School of Public Health, 1984).

3 World Bank, *World Development Report, 1986.*
4 *New Internationalist* (September 1985), p. 128.
5 World Bank, *World Development Report, 1986.*
6 Many of these ideas are developed further by Susan George in *Ill Fares the Land*, ch. 4.

Conclusion

1 US Congressman Tony P. Hall, Democratic Representative for Ohio in the House of Representatives.
2 Philip Alston and Katerina Tomasevski (eds), *The Right to Food* (Netherlands Institute for Human Rights & Martinus Nijhoff, Utrecht, 1984), p. 62.

Appendix 1 Further Reading

It is impossible to give an exhaustive list of publications dealing with the problem of world hunger. For those wishing to find out more about particular areas or topics covered in this book, there can be no better starting point than the increasingly informative literature published by leading aid agencies such as Oxfam, War on Want, CAFOD and Christian Aid in Britain, and the American Council of Voluntary Agencies (ACVA) on behalf of US agencies. Otherwise, the list below contains some important recent publications on the issues of food and poverty.

Periodicals

Useful updated information and general introduction accessible to all age groups can be found in *New Internationalist*, a monthly magazine published in Oxford, England. Also *South* magazine and *Third World Review*, published in London. Recommended magazines on particular areas are *New African*, *Africa Health*, *AfricAsia*, *The Middle East*.

Books

Anne Buchanan, *Food, Poverty and Powers* Spokesman, Nottingham, 1982.
Erik Dammann, *The Future in our Hands* Pergamon, London, 1972.
Susan George, *Feeding the Few: Corporate Control of Food* Institute for Policy Studies, Washington DC, 1976.
Susan George, *How the Other Half Dies: The Real Reasons for World Hunger* Penguin, Harmondsworth, 1976.
Susan George, *Ill Fares the Land* Institute for Policy Studies, Washington DC, 1984.
Susan George and Nigel Paige, *Food for Beginners* Writers and Readers, London, 1982.

Jeremy Hill and Hilary Scannell, *Due South: Socialists and World Development* Pluto Press, London, 1983.

F. Moore Lappé, J. Collins and D. Kinley, *Aid as Obstacle* Institute for Food and Development Policy, San Francisco, 1980.

A. Pearse, *Seeds of Plenty, Seeds of Want* Clarendon Press, Oxford, 1980.

William Shawcross, *The Quality of Mercy* Fontana/Collins, London, 1985.

Nigel Twose, *Cultivating Hunger* Oxfam Publications, Oxford, 1984.

Appendix 2 Useful Addresses

American Council of Voluntary Agencies, 200 Park Avenue South, New York NY 10003, USA.

CAFOD, 2 Garden Close, Stockwell Road, London SW9 9TY.

Cooperative for American Relief Everywhere (CARE), 660 First Avenue, New York, NY 10016, USA.

Christian Aid, P. O. Box 1, London SW9 8BH.

Eritrean Relief Association, BCM Box 865, London WC1V 6XX.

Euro-Action Accord, 3rd Floor, Francis House, Francis Street, London SW1P 1DG.

Inter-Church Coordinating Committee for Development Projects (ICCO), Zusterplein 22A, P. O. Box 151, 3700 AD Zeist, Netherlands.

International Council of Voluntary Agencies (ICVA), 13 Rue Gauthier, Geneva 1201, Switzerland.

International Fund for Agricultural Development (IFAD), 107 Via del Serafico, Rome 00142, Italy.

Intermediate Technology Group, 9 King Street, London WC2E 8HW.

Oxfam, 274 Banbury Road, Oxford.

Relief Society of Tigray, 27 Beresford Road, London N5.

Trocaire, 169 Booterstown Avenue, Blackrock, Co. Dublin, Eire.

War on Want, 37–9 Great Guildford Street, London SE1 0ES.

World Development Movement, Bedford Chambers, Covent Garden, London WC2E X8HA.

Index